C++

THE POCKET REFERENCE

Herbert Schildt

Osborne **McGraw-Hill**

Berkeley New York St. Louis San Francisco
Auckland Bogotá Hamburg London Madrid
Mexico City Milan Montreal New Delhi Panama City
Paris São Paulo Singapore Sydney
Tokyo Toronto

Osborne **McGraw-Hill**
2600 Tenth Street
Berkeley, California 94710
U.S.A.

For information on translations or book distributors outside of the
U.S.A., please write to Osborne **McGraw-Hill** at the above address.

C++ The Pocket Reference

Copyright © 1992 by **McGraw-Hill**, Inc. All rights reserved. Printed in
the United States of America. Except as permitted under the
Copyright Act of 1976, no part of this publication may be reproduced
or distributed in any form or by any means, or stored in a database or
retrieval system, without the prior written permission of the
publisher, with the exception that the program listings may be
entered, stored, and executed in a computer system, but they may
not be reproduced for publication.

Publisher: Kenna S. Wood
Aquisitions Editor: Jeffrey M. Pepper
Associate Editor: Emily R. Rader
Technical Editor: Robin Rowe
Project Editors: Linda Medoff, Paul Medoff
Copy Editor: Paul Medoff
Proofreader: Linda Medoff
Computer Designer: Peter F. Hancik
Cover Design: Bay Graphics Design, Inc.

1234567890 DOC 998765432

ISBN 0-07-881935-0

Information has been obtained by Osborne **McGraw-Hill** from sources believed to be
reliable. However, because of the possibility of human or mechanical error by our
sources, Osborne **McGraw-Hill**, or others, Osborne **McGraw-Hill** does not guarantee
the accuracy, adequacy, or completeness of any information and is not responsible for
any errors or omissions or the results obtained from the use of such information.

Contents

Introduction   v

Data Types and Variables   1

Functions   22

Operators   33

Keyword Summary   50

The C++ Preprocessor   84

The Standard I/O Functions   94

String and Character Functions   128

Mathematical Functions   146

Time, Date, and Other
    System-Related Functions   155

Dynamic Allocation   166

Miscellaneous Functions   170

The C++ Class-Based I/O System . .   187

Introduction

C++ is the expanded and enhanced version of the C language. It was first invented by Bjarne Stroustrup in 1980 while working at Bell Laboratories in Murray Hill, New Jersey. Most additions made to the C language are designed to support object-oriented programming (OOP). However, some features were added to simply improve or expand the C programming environment, so C++ can also be viewed as simply a "better C." For this reason, C++ is widely used for traditional, structured programming in addition to object-oriented programming.

Data Types and Variables

C++ has a rich assortment of built-in data types available to the programmer. In addition, custom data types may be created to fit virtually any need.

The Basic Types

C++ has five basic built-in data types, as shown here:

Type	C++ Keyword Equivalent
character	char
integer	int
floating point	float
double floating point	double
valueless	void

The basic types (with the exception of **void**) may be modified using one or more of the C++ type modifiers:

signed

unsigned

short

long

The type modifiers precede the type name that they modify.

The allowable combinations of the basic types and modifiers are shown in the following table, along with their approximate size and minimum range.

Type	Approximate Size in Bits	Minimal Range
char	8	−127 to 127
unsigned char	8	0 to 255
signed char	8	−127 to 127
int	16	−32767 to 32767
unsigned int	16	0 to 65535
signed int	16	same as int
short int	16	same as int
unsigned short int	16	0 to 65535
signed short int	16	same as short int
long int	32	−2147483647 to 2147483647
signed long int	32	same as long int
unsigned long int	32	0 to 4294967295
float	32	6 digits of precision
double	64	10 digits of precision
long double	128	10 digits of precision

Declaring Variables

Variable names are strings of letters or digits from one to several characters in length. (A digit cannot begin a name, however.) Variable names may be of any length. The underscore may also be used as part of the variable name for clarity, such as **first_time**. Uppercase and lowercase are different. For example, **test** and **TEST** are two different variables.

All variables must be declared prior to use. Here is the general form of the declaration:

type variable_name;

For example, to declare an **x** to be a **float**, **y** to be an integer, and **ch** to be a character, you would type

```
float x;
int y;
char ch;
```

You can declare more than one variable of a type by using a comma-separated list. For example, the following statement declares three integers.

```
int a, b, c;
```

Initializing Variables

A variable can be initialized by following its name with an equal sign and an initial value. For example, this declaration assigns **count** an initial value of 100.

```
int count = 100;
```

In C++, initializers may be any expression that is valid when the variable is declared. This includes other variables and function calls.

Classes

The *class* is C++'s basic unit of encapsulation. It is essentially a collection of variables and functions that manipulate those variables. Its general form is shown here:

```
class tag : inheritance-list {
  // private members by default
  element priv1;
  element priv2;
  // ...
protected:
  // private members that may be inherited
  element prot1;
  element prot2;
  // ...
public:
  // public members
  element pub1;
  element pub2;
  // ...
} object-list;
```

Here, *tag* is the name of the class type. Once the class declaration has been compiled, the *tag* becomes a new data type name that may be used to declare objects of the class. The *object-list* is a comma-separated list of objects of type *tag*. This list is optional. Class objects may be declared later in your program by simply using the tag name. The *inheritance-list* is also optional. When present, it specifies the class or classes that the new class is inheriting.

A class may also include a *constructor function* and a *destructor function*. (Either or both are optional.) A constructor function is called when an object of the class is first created. The destructor is called when an object is destroyed. A constructor function has the same name as the class tag. A destructor function has as its name the tag preceded by a ~ (tilde). In a class hierarchy, constructors are executed in order of derivation and destructors are executed in reverse order.

By default, all elements of a class are private to that class and may only be accessed by other members of that class. To allow an element of the class to be accessed by functions that are not members of the class, you must declare them after the keyword **public**, for example:

```
class myclass {
  int a, b; // private to myclass
public:
  // class members accessible by nonmembers
  void setab(int i, int j) { a = i; b = j; }
  void showab(){ cout << a << ' ' << b <<
                endl; }
} ;

myclass ob1, ob2;
```

This declaration creates a class type, called **myclass**, that contains two private variables, **a** and **b**. It also contains two public functions called **setab()** and **showab()**. The fragment also declares two objects of type **myclass** called **ob1** and **ob2**.

Note A class declaration simply defines a new data type. It does not create any objects of that type (unless some are specified in its object list). An object is an instantiation of a class type, which must be created explicitly using a declaration statement.

When operating on an object of a class, use the dot (.) operator to reference individual elements. The arrow operator (–>) is used when accessing an object using a pointer to it. For example, the following accesses the **putinfo()** function of **entry** using the dot operator and the **show()** function using the arrow operator.

```
struct cl_type {
  int x;
  float f;
public:
  void putinfo(int a, float t) {x = a; f = t; }
  void show(){ cout << a << ' ' << f <<
              endl; }
} ;

cl_type entry, *p;

// ...

entry.putinfo(10, 0.23);

p = &entry; // put entry's address in p

p->show(); // displays entry's data
```

Structures

In C++, a *structure* is the same as a class except that by default, all elements are public. To make an element private, you must use the **private** keyword. The general form of a structure declaration is like this:

```
struct tag {
  // public members by default
  element pub1;
  element pub2;
```

```
  // ...
 protected:
  // private members that may be inherited
  element prot1;
  element prot2;
  // ...
 private:
  // private members
  element priv1;
  element priv2;
  // ...
} object-list;
```

Unions

A *union* is a class type in which all data members share the same memory location. A union may include both member functions and data. A union is like a structure in the sense that by default all of its elements are public. To create private elements, you must use the **private** keyword. The general form for declaration of a union is

```
union tag {
  // public by default
  element 1;
  element 2;
  // ...
private:
  // private data and functions
  element priv1;
  element priv2;
  // ...
} object-list;
```

The elements of a union overlay each other. For example,

```
union tom {
   char ch;
   int x;
} t;
```

declares **union tom**, which looks like this in memory:

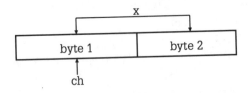

Like a class, the individual variables that comprise the union are referenced using the dot operator. The arrow operator is used with a pointer to a union.

There are several restrictions that apply to unions. First, a union cannot inherit any other class of any type. A union cannot be a base class. A union cannot have virtual member functions. No members may be declared as **static**. A union cannot have as a member any object that overloads the = operator. Finally, no object can be a member of a union if the object has a constructor or destructor function.

There is a special type of union in C++ called an *anonymous union*. An anonymous union declaration does not contain a tag name and there are no objects of that union declared. Instead, an anonymous union simply tells the compiler that member variables of the union are to share the same memory location. However, the variables themselves are referenced directly, without using the normal dot or arrow operator syntax. The variables that make up an anonymous union are at the same scope level as any other variable declared within the same block. This implies that the union variable names must not conflict with any other names valid within their scope. For example, here is an anonymous union:

```
union { // anonymous union
  int a;   // a and f share
  float f; // the same memory location
};

// ...

a = 10; // access a
cout << f; // access f
```

Here, **a** and **f** both share the same memory location. As you can see, the names of the union variables are referenced directly without the use of the dot or arrow operator.

In addition to all restrictions that apply to unions in general, several new restrictions apply. First, anonymous unions must contain only data—no member functions are allowed. Anonymous unions may not contain the **private** keyword. Finally, a global anonymous union must be declared as **static**.

Enumerations

Another type of variable that can be created is called an *enumeration*. An enumeration is a list of named integer constants. Thus, an enumeration type is simply a specification of the list of names that belong to the enumeration.

To create an enumeration requires the use of the keyword **enum**. The general form of an enumeration type is enum *tag* { *list of names* };

The *tag* is the enumeration's type name. The list of named values is comma separated.

For example, the following fragment defines an enumeration of cities called **cities** and the variable **c** of type **cities**. Finally, **c** is assigned the value "Houston".

```
enum cities {Houston, Austin, Amarillo };
cities c;

c = Houston;
```

In an enumeration, the value of the first (leftmost) name is, by default, 0, the second name has the value 1, the third has the value 2, and so on. In general, each name is given a value one greater than the name that precedes it. You can give a name a specific value by adding an initializer. For example, in the following enumeration, **Austin** will have the value 10.

```
enum cities {Houston, Austin=10, Amarillo };
```

In this example, **Amarillo** will have the value 11 because each name will be one greater than the one that precedes it.

The Storage Class Specifiers

The type modifiers **extern**, **auto**, **register**, and **static** are used to alter the way C++ creates storage for variables. These specifiers precede the type that they modify.

extern

If the **extern** modifier is placed before a variable name, the compiler will know that the variable has been declared elsewhere. In essence, **extern** tells the compiler the type of a variable without actually allocating storage for it. The **extern** modifier is most commonly used when there are two or more files sharing the same global variables.

auto

auto tells the compiler that the local variable it precedes is created upon entry into a block and destroyed upon exit from a block. Since all variables defined inside a function are **auto** by default, the **auto** keyword is seldom (if ever) used.

register

When C (the base language for C++) was first invented, the **register** modifier could only be used on local integer or character variables because it caused the compiler to attempt to keep that variable in a register of the CPU instead of placing it in memory. This made all references to that variable extremely fast. However, the ANSI C standard expanded the definition of **register**, and it is this expanded definition that is used by C++. It states that any variable may be specified as **register** and it is the compiler's job to optimize accesses to it. For characters and integers, this still means putting them into a register in the CPU, but for other types of data, it may mean using cache memory, for example. Finally, keep in mind that **register** is only a request. The compiler is free to ignore it. The reason for this is that only so many variables can be optimized for speed.

When this limit is exceeded, the compiler will simply ignore further **register** requests.

static

The **static** modifier instructs the compiler to keep a local variable in existence during the lifetime of the program instead of creating and destroying it each time it comes into and goes out of scope. Therefore, making a function's local variables **static** allows them to maintain their values between function calls.

The **static** modifer may also be applied to global variables. When this is done, it causes that variable's scope to be restricted to the file in which it is declared.

Type Qualifiers

The type qualifiers **const** and **volatile** provide additional information about the variables they precede.

const

Variables of type **const** may not be changed by your program during execution. The compiler is free to place variables of this type into read-only memory (ROM). For example,

```
const int a;
```

will create an integer called **a** that may not be modified by your program. It can, however, be used in other types of expressions. A **const** variable will receive its value either from an explicit initialization or by some hardware-dependent means. The inclusion of **const** type variables aids in the development of ROM-able applications.

volatile

The modifier **volatile** is used to tell the compiler that a variable's value may be changed in ways not explicitly specified by the program. For example, a global variable's address may be passed to the clock routine of the operating system and used to hold the real time of the system. In this situation, the contents of the variable are altered without any explicit assignment statements in the program. This is important because compilers will sometimes automatically optimize certain expressions by making the assumption that the contents of a variable are unchanging inside an expression in order to achieve higher performance. The **volatile** modifier will prevent this optimization in those rare situations where this assumption is not the case.

Addressing Type Modifiers

Many C++ compilers designed for use with the 8086 family of processors (8086, 80186, 80286, 80386, and 80486) have added the following modifiers, which may be applied to pointer declarations to allow explicit control—and override—of the default addressing mode used to compile your program.

_cs _ds _es _ss
far near huge

The 8086, 80186, and 80286 use a segmented memory architecture with a total address space of one megabyte. (The 80386 and 80486 use the same scheme when operating in 8086 emulation mode.) However, this one megabyte is divided into 64K *segments*. The 8086 can directly access any byte within a segment and does so with a 16-bit register. Therefore, the address of any specific byte within the computer is the combination of the segment and the 16-bit *offset*. The segment specifies which 64K region of memory is being used and the 16-bit address identifies the specific byte within that segment. The segments must start on addresses that are even multiples of 16.

The 8086 has four segment registers: one for code, one for data, one for the stack, and one extra segment. These registers are, respectively, CS, DS, SS, and ES. Each segment register is 16 bits wide.

The 8086 only loads a 16-bit offset to access memory within the segment already loaded into one of its segment registers. However, if you wish to access memory outside that segment, both the segment register and the offset must be loaded with the proper values. This effectively means that a 32-bit address is required. The difference between the two is that it takes twice as long to load two 16-bit registers as it does to load one. Hence your programs run much slower. The exact way the program will run slower is determined by the memory model that the program uses.

Most C++ compilers for the 8086 family of processors can compile your program six different ways, and each organizes the memory in the computer differently. The model used affects the execution speed of your program. The six models are called tiny, small, medium, compact, large, and huge. They are described here.

Tiny Model

The tiny model compiles a program so that all the segment registers are set to the same value and all addressing is done using 16 bits. This means that the code, data, and stack must all be within the same 64K segment. This method of compilation produces the smallest, fastest code. Programs compiled using this version may be converted into .COM files.

Small Model

In the small model, all addressing is done using only the 16-bit offset. The code segment is separate from the data, stack, and extra segments, which are in their own segment. This means that the total size of a program compiled this way is 128K split between code and data. The addressing time is the same as that for the tiny model, but the program can be twice as big.

Medium Model

The medium model is for large programs where the code exceeds the one-segment restriction of the small model. Here, the code may use multiple segments and requires 32-bit addresses, but the stack, data, and extra segments are in their own segment and use 16-bit addresses. This is good for use with large programs that require little data.

Compact Model

The complement of the medium model is the compact model. In this version, program code is restricted to one segment, but data may occupy several segments. This means that all accesses to data require 32-bit addressing but the code uses 16-bit addressing. This is good for programs that require large amounts of data but little code.

Large Model

The large model allows both code and data to use multiple segments. However, the largest single item of data, such as an array, is limited to 64K. This model is used when you have both large code and data requirements. It also runs much slower than any of the previous versions.

Huge Model

The huge model is the same as the large model with the exception that individual data items may exceed 64K. This makes run-time speed degrade further.

Overriding a Memory Model

The addressing modifiers may only be applied to pointers or to functions. When they are applied to pointers, they affect the way data is accessed. When applied to functions, they affect the way the function is called and returned from.

The address modifier follows the base type and precedes the variable name. For example, this declares a **far** pointer called **f_pointer**.

```
char far *f_pointer;
```

When an address modifier is used, it causes the compiler to use the specified addressing mode rather than the default mode.

Arrays

You may declare arrays of any data type. The general form of a singly dimensioned array is

type var-name[*size*];

where *type* specifies the data type of each element in the array and *size* specifies the number of elements in the array. For example, to declare an integer array **x** of 100 elements you would write

```
int x[100];
```

This will create an array that is 100 elements long with the first element being 0 and the last being 99. For example, the following loop will load the numbers 0 through 99 into array **x**.

```
for(t=0;t<100; t++) x[t]=t;
```

You may declare arrays of any valid data type, including classes that you create.

Multidimensional arrays are declared by placing the additional dimensions inside additional brackets. For example, to declare a 10 × 20 integer array you would write

```
int x[10][20];
```

Remember In C++, all array indexes begin at 0. Further, C++ provides no array bounds checking. Such safety checks are your responsibility.

typedef

You can create a new name for an existing type using **typedef**. Its general form is

typedef *type newname*;

For example, the following tells the compiler that **feet** is another name for **int**:

```
typedef int feet;
```

Now, the following declaration is perfectly legal and creates an integer variable called **distance**.

```
feet distance;
```

Constants

In C++, *constants* refer to fixed values that may not be altered by the program.

C++ constants can be of any of the basic data types. The way each constant is represented depends upon its type. Character constants are enclosed between single quotes. For example 'a' and '%' are both character constants. Integer constants are specified as numbers without fractional components. For example, 10 and –100 are integer constants. Floating point constants require the use of the decimal point followed by the number's fractional component. For example, 11.123 is a floating point constant. C++ also allows you to use scientific notation for floating point numbers.

There are two floating point types: **float** and **double**. Also, there are several flavors of the basic types that are generated using the type modifiers. By default, the compiler fits a numeric constant into the smallest compatible data type that will hold it. Therefore, 10 is an **int** by default, but 60000 is **unsigned** and 100000 is a **long**. Even though the value 10 could be fit into a character, the compiler will not do this because it means crossing type boundaries. The only exceptions to the smallest type rule are floating point constants, which are assumed to be of type **double**. For many programs, the compiler defaults are perfectly adequate. However, it is possible to specify precisely the type of constant you want.

In cases where the default assumption that C++ makes about a numeric constant is not what you want, C++ allows you to specify the exact type of numeric constant by using a suffix. For floating point types, if you follow the number with an F, the number is treated as a **float**. If you follow it with an L, the number becomes a **long double**. For integer types, the U suffix stands for **unsigned** and the L for **long**. Some examples are shown here:

Data Type	Constant Examples
int	1 123 21000 −234
long int	35000L −34L
unsigned int	10000U 987U
float	123.23F 4.34e−3F
double	123.23 12312333 −0.9876324
long double	1001.2L

Hexadecimal and Octal Constants

It is sometimes easier to use a number system based on 8 or 16 instead of 10. The number system based on 8 is called *octal* and uses the digits 0 through 7. In octal the number 10 is the same as 8 in decimal. The base 16 number system is called *hexadecimal* and uses the digits 0 through 9 plus the letters A through F, which stand for 10, 11, 12, 13, 14, and 15. For example, the hexadecimal number 10 is 16 in decimal. Because of the frequency with which these two number systems are used, C++ allows you to specify integer constants in hexadecimal or octal instead of decimal if you prefer. A hexadecimal constant must begin with a 0x (a zero followed by an x) then the constant in hexadecimal form. An octal constant begins with a zero. Here are two examples:

```
int hex = 0x80;    /* 128 in decimal */

int oct = 012;     /* 10 in decimal */
```

String Constants

C++ supports one other type of constant in addition to those of the predefined data types: *string*. A string is a set of characters enclosed by double quotes. For example, "this is a test" is a string. You must not confuse strings with characters. A single character constant is enclosed by single quotes, such as 'a'. However, "a" is a string containing only one letter. String constants are automatically null terminated by the compiler.

Backslash Character Constants

Enclosing character constants in single quotes works for most printing characters, but a few, such as the carriage return, are impossible to enter into your program's source code from the keyboard. For this reason, C++ recognizes several *backslash character constants*. These constants are listed here:

Code	Meaning
\b	Backspace
\f	Form feed
\n	Newline
\r	Carriage return
\t	Horizontal tab
\"	Double quote
\'	Single quote
\0	Null
\\	Backslash
\v	Vertical tab
\a	Alert
\N	Octal constant (where N is an octal constant)
\xN	Hexadecimal constant (where N is a hexadecimal constant)

The backslash constants can be used anywhere a character can. For example, the following statement outputs a newline and a tab and then prints the string "This is a test".

```
cout << "\n\tThis is a test";
```

Functions

A C++ program is a collection of one or more user-defined functions. One of the functions must be called **main()** because it is at this function where execution will begin. Traditionally, **main()** is usually the first function in a program; however, it can go anywhere in the program.

The general form of a C++ function is

type function_name (parameter list)
{
 body of function
}

The *parameter list* is a comma-separated list of variables that will receive any arguments passed to the function. If the function has no parameters, no parameter declaration is needed. For example, the following function has two integer parameters called **i** and **j** and a **double** parameter called **count**.

```
void fn1(int i, int j, double count)
{ ...
```

Notice that you must declare each parameter separately.

The function's return type declaration is optional—if no explicit type declaration is present, the function defaults to integer. Functions terminate and return automatically to the calling procedure when the last brace is encountered. You may force a return prior to that by using the **return** statement.

All functions, except those declared as **void**, return a value. The type of the return value must match the type declaration of the function. If no explicit type declaration has been made, the return value is defaulted to integer.

If a **return** statement is part of a non-**void** function, then the return value of the function is the value in the **return** statement.

Function Overloading

In C++, functions may be overloaded. When a function is overloaded, two or more functions share the same name. However, each version of an overloaded function must have a different number and/or type of parameters. (The function return types may also differ, but this is not necessary.) When an overloaded function is called, the compiler decides which version of the function to use based upon the type and/or number of arguments, calling the function that has the closest match.

Default Arguments

You may assign a function parameter a default value, which will be automatically used when no corresponding argument is specified when the function is called. The default value is specified in a manner syntactically similar to a variable initialization. For example, this function assigns its two parameters default values:

```
void myfunc(int a = 0, int b = 10)
{ // ...
```

Given the default arguments, **myfunc()** can be legally called in these three ways:

```
myfunc(); // a defaults to 0; b defaults to 10
```

or

```
myfunc(-1); // a is passed -1; b defaults to 10
```

or

```
myfunc(-1, 99); // a is passed -1; b is 99
```

When you create functions that have default arguments, you must specify the default values only once: either in the function prototype or in its definition. (You cannot specify them each place, even if you use the same values.) Generally, default values are specified in the prototype.

When giving a function default arguments remember that you must specify all nondefaulting arguments first. Once you begin to specify default arguments, there may be no intervening nondefaulting ones.

Prototypes

In C++, all functions must be prototyped. The general form of a prototype is shown here:

```
type name(parameter list);
```

In essence, a *prototype* is simply the return type, name, and parameter list of a function's definition, followed by a semicolon.

The following example shows how the function **fn()** is prototyped.

```
float fn(float x); /* prototype */
```

```
        .
        .
// function definition
float fn(float x)
{
  // ...
}
```

To specify the prototype for a function that takes a variable number of arguments, use three periods at the point at which the variable number of parameters begin. For example, the **printf()** function could be prototyped like this:

```
int printf(const char *format, ...);
```

When specifying the prototype to an overloaded function, each version of that function must have its own prototype.

The Scope and Lifetime of Variables

C++ has two general classes of variables: *global* and *local*. A *global variable* is available for use by all functions in the program, while a *local variable* is known and used only by the function in which it is declared. In some C++ literature, global variables are referred to as *external variables* and local variables are called *dynamic* or *automatic* variables. This pocket reference will use local and global because they are the more commonly used terms.

A global variable must be declared outside of all functions, including the **main()** function. Global variables are generally placed at the top of the file, prior to **main()**, for ease of reading and because a variable must be declared before it is used. A local variable is declared at any point inside a function after the function's opening brace. For example, the following program declares one global variable, **x**, and two local variables, **x** and **y**.

```
#include <iostream.h>

int f1(void);
int x;

main(void)
{
  int y;

  y = f1();
  x = 100;
  cout << x << ' ' << x*y;

  return 0;
}

f1(void)
{
  int x;

  cin >> x;
  return x;
}
```

This program will multiply the number entered from the keyboard by 100. Note that the local variable **x** in **f1()** has no relationship to the global variable **x**. This is because local variables that have the same name as global variables always take precedence over the global variables.

In C++, local variables may be declared anywhere inside a block. (This differs from C, in which local variables must be declared at the start of each block, prior to the first "action" statement.) This means that local variables can be declared near where they are used, helping to avoid accidental misuse.

Global variables stay in existence the entire duration of the program, while local variables are created when the function is entered and destroyed when the function is exited. This means that local variables do not hold their values between function calls. You can use the **static** modifier, however, to preserve values between calls.

The formal parameters to a function are also local variables and, aside from their job of receiving the value of the calling arguments, behave and can be used like any other local variable.

The main() Function

All C++ programs must have a **main()** function. When execution begins, this is the first function called. You must not have more than one function called **main()**. When **main()** terminates, the program is over and control passes back to the operating system.

At least two parameters are allowed to **main()**. They are **argc** and **argv**. (Some compilers will allow additional parameters.) These two variables will hold the number of command-line arguments and a pointer to them respectively.

Command-line arguments are the information that you type in after the program name when you execute a program. For example, when you compile a C++ program you type something like this:

```
CC MYPROG.CPP
```

where MYPROG.CPP is the name of the program that you wish to compile, and it is also a command-line argument to CC.

argc is an integer and its value will always be at least 1 because the program name is the first argument as far as C++ is concerned. **argv** must be declared as an array of character pointers. Their usage is shown below in a short program that will print your name on the screen.

```
#include <iostream.h>

main(int argc, char *argv[])
{
  if(argc<2)
    cout << "enter your name.\n";
  else
    cout << "hello " << argv[1];

  return 0;
}
```

Reference Parameters

In C++ it is possible to automatically pass the address of a variable to a function. This is accomplished using a *reference parameter.*

By default, all arguments are passed to a function using the call-by-value parameter passing mechanism. Using this method, a copy of the value of each argument is made and then passed to the function. In this situation, the function operates on the copy of the argument and does not affect the variable used in the call. However, by using a reference parameter, C++ will automatically create a call by reference (sometimes referred to as a call by address). In this case, the address of an argument is passed to the function and the function operates on the argument, not a copy.

To create a reference parameter, precede its name with the **&** (ampersand). Inside the function, you may use the parameter normally, without any need to use the * (asterisk) operator. The compiler will automatically dereference the address for you. For example, the following creates a function called **swap()** that uses two reference parameters to exchange the values of its two arguments.

```
void swap(int &i, int &j)
{
   int t;

   t = i;
   i = j;
   j = t;
}
```

When invoking **swap()**, you simply use the normal function-call syntax. For example:

```
int a=10, b=20;

swap(a, b); // exchange a and b
```

Because **i** and **j** are reference parameters, the address of **a** and **b** are automatically generated and passed to the function. Inside the function, the parameter names are used without any need for the * operator because the compiler automatically refers to the calling arguments each time **i** and **j** are used.

Constructors and Destructors

A class may contain a constructor function, a destructor function, or both. A constructor is called when an object of the class is first created and the destructor is called when an object of the class is destroyed. A constructor has the same name as the class that it is a member of and the destructor's name is the same as its class, except that it is preceded by a ~. Neither constructors nor destructors have return values.

Constructor functions may have parameters. You can use these parameters to pass values to a constructor function, which can be used to initialize an object. The arguments that are passed to the parameters are specified when each object is created. For example, this fragment illustrates how to pass a constructor an argument:

```
class myclass {
   int a;
public:
   myclass(int i) {a = i; } // constructor
   ~myclass() {cout << "Destructing..."; }
};

// ...

myclass ob(3); // pass 3 to i
```

When **ob** is declared, the value 3 is passed to the constructor's parameter **i**, which is then assigned to **a**.

Linkage Specification

Because it is common to link a C++ function with functions generated by another language, C++ allows you to specify a *linkage specification* that tells the compiler how to link a function. It has this general form:

extern "*language*" *function-prototype*

where *language* denotes the language to which you want the function to link. To declare several functions using the same linkage specification, you can use this general form:

extern "*language*" {
function-prototypes
}

The C++ Standard Library

Like C, C++ does not have built-in functions to perform disk I/O, console I/O, and a number of other useful procedures. The way these things are accomplished in C++ is by using a set of predefined library functions that are supplied with the compiler. This library is usually called the "Standard Library."

Most C++ compilers come with a very extensive function library. Many of the functions are specific to a certain environment or compiler and are not portable. However, all C++ compilers will minimally support the library of functions defined by the ANSI C standard. The prototypes for these standard functions are found in *header files*, which you must include with your program.

The header files that are defined by the ANSI C standard are shown here:

Header File	Purpose
ASSERT.H	Defines the **assert()** macro
CTYPE.H	Supports character handling
ERRNO.H	Supports error reporting
FLOAT.H	Defines implementation-dependent floating point values
LIMITS.H	Defines various implementation-dependent limits
LOCALE.H	Supports the **setlocale()** function
MATH.H	Contains various definitions used by the math library
SETJMP.H	Supports nonlocal jumps
SIGNAL.H	Defines signal values
STDARG.H	Supports variable-length argument lists
STDDEF.H	Defines some commonly used constants
STDIO.H	Supports file I/O
STDLIB.H	Contains miscellaneous declarations
STRING.H	Supports string functions
TIME.H	Supports system time functions

In addition to the standard library functions, all C++ compilers will supply certain class libraries. While there is currently no standard that specifies what class libraries must be supplied, all C++ compilers will support the C++ I/O system. Specifically, all C++ compilers will contain class libraries to support general I/O, file I/O, and in-RAM I/O. The header files required by these libraries are IOSTREAM.H, FSTREAM.H, and STRSTREAM.H, respectively.

Operators

C++ has a very rich set of operators that can be divided into the following classes: arithmetic, relational and logical, bitwise, pointer, assignment, I/O, and miscellaneous.

Arithmetic Operators

C++ has the following seven arithmetic operators:

Operator	Action
−	Subtraction, unary minus
+	Addition
*	Multiplication
/	Division
%	Modulus division
− −	Decrement
+ +	Increment

The +, −, *, and / operators work in the expected fashion. The % operator returns the remainder of an integer division. The increment and decrement operators increase or decrease the operand by one.

These operators have the following order of precedence:

Precedence	Operators
Highest	++ −− − (unary minus)
	* / %
Lowest	+ −

Operators on the same precedence level are evaluated left to right.

Relational and Logical Operators

The relational and logical operators are used to produce true/false results and are often used together. In C++, *any* nonzero number evaluates as true. The only value that is false is 0. The relational and logical operators are listed here:

Relational Operators

Operator	Meaning
>	Greater than
>=	Greater than or equal
<	Less than
<=	Less than or equal
==	Equal
!=	Not equal

Logical Operators

Operator	Meaning
&&	AND
||	OR
!	NOT

The relational operators are used to compare two values. The logical operators are used to connect two values or, in the case of NOT, to reverse a value. The precedence of these operators is shown here:

Precedence	Operators
Highest	!
	> >= < <=
	== !=
	&&
Lowest	||

As an example, the following **if** statement evaluates to true and prints the line **X is less than 10**:

```
X = 9;
if(X < 10) cout << "X is less than 10";
```

However, in the following example, no message is displayed because both operands associated with AND must be true for the outcome to be true.

```
X = 9;
Y = 9;
if(X < 10 && Y > 10)
    cout << "X is less than 10; Y is greater";
```

The Bitwise Operators

Unlike most other programming languages, C++ provides operators that operate on the actual bits inside a variable. The bitwise operators can only be used on integers or characters. The bitwise operators are

Operator	Meaning
&	AND
|	OR
^	XOR
~	One's complement
>>	Right shift
<<	Left shift

AND, OR, and XOR

The truth tables for AND, OR, and XOR are

&	0	1
0	0	0
1	0	1

|	0	1
0	0	1
1	1	1

^	0	1
0	0	1
1	1	0

These rules are applied to each bit in a byte when the bitwise AND, OR, and XOR operations are performed.

For example, a sample AND operation is shown here:

```
  0 1 0 0   1 1 0 1
& 0 0 1 1   1 0 1 1
---------------------
  0 0 0 0   1 0 0 1
```

An OR operation looks like this:

```
  0 1 0 0   1 1 0 1
| 0 0 1 1   1 0 1 1
---------------------
  0 1 1 1   1 1 1 1
```

An XOR operation is shown here:

```
  0 1 0 0   1 1 0 1
^ 0 0 1 1   1 0 1 1
---------------------
  0 1 1 1   0 1 1 0
```

The One's Complement Operator

The one's complement operator, ~, will invert all the bits in a byte. For example, if a character variable, **ch**, has the bit pattern

```
0 0 1 1   1 0 0 1
```

then

```
ch = ~ch;
```

places the bit pattern

```
1 1 0 0   0 1 1 0
```

into **ch**.

The Shift Operators

The right (>>) and left (<<) shift operators shift all bits in a byte or a word the specified amount. As bits are shifted 0's are brought in. (If the value being shifted is a negative, signed number and a right shift is performed, then 1's are shifted in to preserve the sign.) The number on the right side of the shift operator specifies the number of positions to shift. The general form of each shift operator is

variable >> number of bit positions

variable << number of bit positions

Given this bit pattern (and assuming an unsigned value),

```
0 0 1 1   1 1 0 1
```

a shift right yields

```
0 0 0 1   1 1 1 0
```

while a shift left produces

```
0 1 1 1   1 0 1 0
```

A shift right is effectively a division by 2, and a shift left is a multiplication by 2. The following code fragment will first multiply and then divide the value in **x**.

```
int x;

x = 10;
x = x<<1;
x = x>>1;
```

Because of the way negative numbers are represented inside the machine, you must be careful if you try to use a shift for multiplication or division. Moving a 1 into the most significant bit position will make the computer think that it is a negative number.

The precedence of the bitwise operators is shown here:

Precedence	Operators
Highest	~
	>> <<
	&
	^
Lowest	|

Pointer Operators

The two pointer operators are ***** and **&**. It is unfortunate that these operators use the same symbols as the multiplication operator and the bitwise AND because they have nothing in common with them. In simple terms, a *pointer* is a variable that contains the address of another variable. Or, in different terms, the variable that contains the address of the other is said to "point to" the other variable.

The & Pointer Operator

The **&** operator returns the address of the variable it precedes. For example, if the integer **x** is located at memory address 1000, then

```
y = &x;
```

places the value 1000 into **y**. The **&** can be thought of as "the address of". For example, the previous statement could be read as "place the address of x into y".

The * Pointer Operator

The * is the *indirection operator*. It uses the current value of the variable it precedes as the address at which data will be stored or obtained. For example, the following fragment

```
y = &x; /* put address of x into y */

*y = 100; /* use address contained in y */
```

places the value 100 into **x**. The * can be remembered as "at address". In this example, it could be read, "place the value 100 at address **y**". Since **y** contains the address of **x**, the value 100 is actually stored in **x**. In words, **y** is said to "point to" **x**. The * operator can also be used on the right-hand side of an assignment. For example,

```
y = &x;

*y = 100;

z = *y/10;
```

places the value of 10 into **z**.

Assignment Operators

In C++, the assignment operator is the single equal sign. However, C++ allows a very convenient form of "shorthand" for assignments of this general type:

variable1 = variable1 operator expression;

Here are two examples:

```
x = x+10;

y = y/z;
```

Assignments of this type can be shortened to

variable1 operator = *expression*;

or, specifically, in the case of the examples above:

```
x += 10;

y /= z;
```

The ? Operator

The **?** operator is a *ternary operator* (it works on three expressions) that is used to replace **if-else** statements of this general type:

if *expression1* then *x* = *expression2*

else *x* = *expression3*

The general form of the **?** operator is

variable = *expression1* ? *expression2* : *expression3*;

If *expression1* is true, then the value assigned is that of *expression2;* otherwise it is the value of *expression3.* For example,

```
x = (y<10) ? 20 : 40;
```

will assign **x** the value of 20 if **y** is less than 10 and 40 if it is not.

The reason that this operator exists, beyond saving typing on your part, is that the compiler can produce very fast code for this statement—much faster than for the similar **if-else** statement.

Member Operators

The . (dot) operator and the –> (arrow) operator are used to reference individual members of classes, structures, and unions. The dot operator is applied to the actual object. The arrow operator is used with a pointer to an object. For example, given the following structure:

```
struct date_time {
  char date[16];
  int time;
} tm;
```

to assign the value "3/12/88" to element **date** of object **tm**, you would write

```
strcpy(tm.date, "3/12/88");
```

However, if **p_tm** is a pointer to an object of type **date_time**, the following statement is used.

```
strcpy(p_tm->date, "3/12/88");
```

The Comma Operator

The comma operator is used most often in the **for** statement. Its effect is to cause a sequence of operations to be performed. The value of the entire expression is the value of the last expression of the comma-separated list. For example, after execution of the following fragment,

```
y=10;

x = (y=y-5,25/y);
```

x will have the value 5 because **y**'s original value of 10 is reduced by 5 and then that value is divided into 25, yielding 5 as the result. You can think of the comma operator as meaning "do this and this" and so on.

sizeof

Although **sizeof** is also considered a keyword, it is a compile-time operator used to determine the size, in bytes, of a variable or data type, including classes, structures, and unions. If used with a type, the type name must be enclosed by parentheses.

For most PC-based C++ compilers, the following example prints the number 2:

```
int x;

cout << sizeof x;
```

The Cast

A *cast* is a special operator that forces one data type to be converted into another. The general form is

(*type*) *expression*

where *type* is the desired data type.

For example, the following cast causes the outcome of the specified integer division to be of type **double**:

```
double d;

d = (double) 10/3;
```

The I/O Operators

In C++, the << and the >> are overloaded to perform I/O operations. When used in an expression in which the left operand is a stream, the >> is an input operator, and the << is an output operator. In the langauge of C++, the >> is called an *extractor* because it *extracts* data from the input stream. The << is called an *inserter* because it *inserts* data into the output stream. The general form of these operators is shown here:

input-stream >> *variable*;

output-stream << *expression*

For example, the following statement inputs two integer variables:

```
int i, j;

cin >> i >> j;
```

The following statement displays "This is a test 10 20":

```
cout << "This is a test " << 10 << 4*5;
```

Overloading the I/O Operators

The << and the >> are overloaded in C++ to perform I/O operations on C++'s built-in types. It is also possible for you to overload these operators so that they perform I/O operations on types that you create.

All overloaded inserter functions have this general form:

```
ostream &operator<<(ostream &stream, class_type obj)
{
  // body of inserter
  return stream;
}
```

Notice that the function returns a reference to a stream of type **ostream**. (**ostream** is the class derived from the **ios** class, which supports output.) Further, the first parameter to the function is a reference to the output stream. The second parameter is the object being inserted. Often the second parameter will also be a reference. The last thing the inserter must do before exiting is return *stream*. The reason for this is to allow the inserter to be used by a chain of insertions.

Extractors are the complements of inserters. The general form of an extractor function is shown here:

```
istream &operator>>(istream &stream, class_type &obj)
{
  // body of extractor
  return stream;
}
```

Extractors return a reference to a stream of type **istream**, which is an input stream. The first parameter must also be a reference to a stream of type **istream**. Notice that the second parameter must be a reference to an object of the class for which the extractor is overloaded. The reason for this is that the object will be modified by the input (extraction) operation.

Note Overloaded inserters and extractors must be either friend functions or stand-alone functions. Neither may not be a member of a class.

The .* and –>* Pointer to Member Operators

C++ allows you to generate a special type of pointer that "points" generically to a public member of a class, not to a specific instance of that member in an object. This sort of pointer is called a *pointer to a member*. A pointer to a member is not the same as a normal C++ pointer. Instead, a pointer to a member provides only an offset into an object of the member's class at which that member can be found. Since member pointers are not true pointers, the . and –> operators cannot be applied to them. To access a member of a class given a pointer to it, you must use the special pointer-to-member operators .* and –>*. They allow you to access a member of a class given a pointer to that member.

When you are accessing a member of an object given an object or a reference to an object, use the .* operator. When accessing a member given a pointer to an object, use the –>* operator.

A pointer to a member is declared by using the general form shown here:

type p_var class-name::*member-name;*

Here, *type* is the base type of the member, *p_var* is the name of the member pointer being declared, *class-name* is the name of the class, and *member-name* is the name of the member.

Here is a short example that demonstrates the .* operator. Pay special attention to the way the member pointers are declared.

```
#include <iostream.h>

class cl {
public:
  cl(int i) {val=i;}
  int val;
  int double_val() {return val+val;}
};

main()
{
  int cl::*data; // data member pointer
  int (cl::*func)(); // func member pointer
  cl ob1(1), ob2(2); // create objects

  data = &cl::val; // get offset of val
  func = &cl::double_val;  // get offset

  cout << "Here are values: ";
  cout << ob1.*data << " " << ob2.*data << "\n";

  cout << "Here they are doubled: ";
  cout << (ob1.*func)() << " ";
  cout << (ob2.*func)() << "\n";

  return 0;
}
```

The :: Scope Resolution Operator

The ::*scope resolution operator* specifies the scope to
which a member belongs. It has this general form:

class-name::*member-name*

Here, *class-name* is the name of the class type that
contains the member specified by *member-name*. Put

differently, *class-name* specifies the scope within which can be found the identifier specified by *member-name*.

To reference the global scope, you do not specify a class name.

new and delete

new and **delete** are C++'s dynamic allocation operators. They are also keywords. See the "Keyword Summary" for details.

Operator Precedence Summary

The table below lists the precedence of all C++ operators. Please note that all operators, except the unary operators and **?**, associate from left to right. The unary operators, *****, **&**, **−**, and the **?** operator associate from right to left.

Precedence	Operators
Highest	() [] −> :: .
	! ~ ++ − − − (type) * & sizeof new delete
	.* −>*
	* / %
	+ −
	<< >>
	< <= > >=
	== ! =

Precedence	Operators
	&
	∧
	|
	&&
	||
	?:
	= += −= *= /= %= >>= <<= &= ∧= |=
Lowest	,

Keyword Summary

C++ adds 17 keywords to those defined by its base language, C. The 32 keywords that form the C language are

auto	double	int	struct
break	else	long	switch
case	enum	register	typedef
char	extern	return	union
const	float	short	unsigned
continue	for	signed	void
default	goto	sizeof	volatile
do	if	static	while

To these, C++ adds the following:

asm	inline	protected	try
catch	new	public	virtual
class	operator	template	
delete	overload	this	
friend	private	throw	

Of these, **catch, try**, and **throw** are experimental and reserved for the future. The keyword **template** might not be accepted by all compilers. **new** and **delete** are both keywords and operators. Finally, **overload** is obsolete and is still accepted simply for backward compatibility.

In addition to the standard C++ keywords, compilers designed for use on an 8086 family processor have added the following keywords to allow greater control over the ways that memory and other system resources are used.

cdecl	_es	interrupt	_ss
_cs	far	near	
_ds	huge	pascal	

All keywords are lowercase.

A brief synopsis of the keywords follows.

asm

asm is used to embed assembly language directly into your C++ program. The general form of the **asm** statement is shown here:

asm ("*instruction*");

Here, *instruction* is the assembly language instruction, which is passed directly to the compiler for assembly in your program.

Many C++ compilers, including Turbo/Borland and Microsoft, allow additional forms of the **asm** statement. For example, both Turbo/Borland and Microsoft allow the following **asm** statements:

```
asm instruction;

asm {
  instruction sequence
}
```

Here, *instruction sequence* is a list of assembly language instructions.

auto

auto is used to declare local variables. However, since its use is completely optional, it is seldom used.

break

break is used to exit from a **do**, **for**, or **while** loop, bypassing the normal loop condition. It is also used to exit from a **switch** statement.

An example of **break** in a loop is shown here:

```
while(x<100) {
  cin >> x;
  if(x < 0) break;  /* terminate if negative */
  process(x);
}
```

Here, if **x** is negative, the loop is terminated.

A **break** always terminates the innermost **for**, **do**, **while**, or **switch** statement, regardless of the way these might be nested. In a **switch** statement, **break** effectively keeps program execution from "falling through" to the next **case**. (Refer to the **switch** statement for details.)

case

One of the options used with a **switch** statement. See **switch**.

catch

catch is experimental. Its purpose is to intercept an exception generated by **throw**, another experimental feature. Check your compiler's user manual for details.

cdecl

The **cdecl** keyword is not part of standard C++. It forces the compiler to compile a function so that its parameter passing conforms with the standard C calling convention. It is found in compilers that allow a Pascal calling convention to be specified. It is then used when you are compiling an entire file using the Pascal option and you want a specific function to be compatible with C/C++.

char

char is a data type used to declare character variables.

class

class is used to declare classes—C++'s basic unit of encapsulation. Its general form is shown here:

class *tag* : *inheritance-list* {
  // private members by default
protected:
  // private members that may be inherited
public:
  // public members
} *object-list*;

Here, *tag* is the name of the new data type being generated by the **class** declaration. The *inheritance-list*, which is optional, specifies any base classes inherited by the new class. By default, elements of a class are private. They may be made protected or public through the use of the **protected** and **public** keywords, respectively.

The *object-list* is optional. If not present, a class declaration simply specifies the form of a class. It does not create any objects of the class.

Note See "Data Types and Variables" for additional information.

const

The **const** modifier tells the compiler that the variable that follows may not be modified. A **const** variable may, however, be given an initial value when it is declared.

continue

continue is used to bypass portions of code in a loop and force the conditional test to be performed. For example, the following **while** loop will simply read characters from the keyboard until an s is typed.

```
while(ch=cin.get()) {
  .if(ch != 's') continue;  /* read another char */
  process(ch);
}
```

The call to **process()** will not occur until **ch** contains the character 's'.

_cs, _ds, _es, _ss

The **_cs**, **_ds**, **_es**, **_ss** modifiers tell the compiler which segment register to use when evaluating a pointer. These modifiers are not standard and apply only to compilers designed for the 8086 family of processors.

For example, this instructs the compiler to use the extra segment when using **ptr**:

```
int _es *ptr;
```

Frankly, there will be few, if any, times that you will need to use these segment register overrides.

default

default is used in the **switch** statement to signal a default block of code to be executed if no matches are found in the **switch**. (See **switch**.)

delete

The **delete** dynamic allocation operator frees the memory pointed to by its argument. This memory must have previously been allocated using **new**. The general form of **delete** is

delete *p_var*;

where *p_var* is a pointer to previously allocated memory.

do

The **do** loop is one of three loop constructs available in C++. The general form of the **do** loop is

do {
  statement block
} while(*condition*);

If only one statement is repeated, the braces are not necessary, but they do add clarity to the statement.

The **do** loop is the only loop in C++ that will always have at least one iteration because the condition is tested at the bottom of the loop.

double

double is a data type specifier used to declare double-precision floating point variables.

else

See **if**.

enum

The **enum** type specifier is used to create enumeration types. An enumeration is simply a list of named integer constants. Hence, an enumeration type specifies what that list consists of. The general form of an enumeration is shown here:

enum *tag* {*name-list*} *var-list*;

The *tag* is the type name of the enumeration. The *var-list* is optional, and enumeration variables may be declared separately from the type definition, as the following example shows. This code declares an enumeration called **color** and a variable of that type called **c**, and it performs an assignment and a conditional test.

```
enum color {red, green, yellow};
color c;

main(void)
{
  c = red;
```

```
    if(c==red) cout << "is red\n";

    return 0;
}
```

For more information on enumerations refer to
Enumerations in the "Data Types and Variables" section.

extern

extern is a data type modifier used to tell the compiler
that a variable is declared elsewhere in the program.
This is often used in conjunction with separately
compiled files that share the same global data and are
linked together. In essence, it notifies the compiler about
the type of a variable without redeclaring it.

As an example, if **first** were declared in another file as
an integer, the following declaration would be used in
subsequent files:

```
extern int first;
```

far

The **far** type modifier is not part of standard C++. It is
used by compilers designed for use on the 8086 family of
processors to force a pointer variable to use 32-bit,
rather than 16-bit, addressing.

float

float is a data type specifier used to declare floating point variables.

for

The **for** loop allows automatic initialization and incrementation of a counter variable. The general form is

for(*initialization*; *condition*; *increment*) {
 statement block
}

If the *statement block* is only one statement, the braces are not necessary.

Although the **for** allows a number of variations, generally the *initialization* is used to set a counter variable to its starting value. The *condition* is generally a relational statement that checks the counter variable against a termination value, and *increment* increments (or decrements) the counter variable.

It is important to understand that if the *condition* is false to begin with, the body of the **for** loop will not execute even once.

The following statement will print the message "hello" ten times.

```
for(t=0; t<10; t++) cout << "hello\n";
```

friend

The keyword **friend** is used to grant a nonmember function access to the private parts of a class. To specify a friend function, include that function's prototype in the public section of a class declaration and precede the entire prototype with the keyword **friend**. For example, in the following class, **myfunc()** is a friend, not a member, of **myclass**.

```
class myclass {
  // ...
public:
  friend void myfunc(int a, float b);
  // ...
};
```

Keep in mind that a **friend** function does not have a **this** pointer because it is not a member of the class.

goto

The **goto** keyword causes program execution to "jump" to the label specified in the **goto** statement. The general form of **goto** is

goto *label*;
.
.
.
label:

All labels must end in a colon and must not conflict with keywords or function names. Furthermore, a **goto** can only branch within the current function—not from one function to another.

huge

The **huge** type modifier is not part of standard C++. It is used by compilers designed for use on the 8086 family of processors to force a pointer variable to use 32- rather than 16-bit addressing. It also allows the object pointed to by a **huge** pointer to be larger than one segment (64K).

if

The **if** keyword allows a course of action to be based on the truth of a condition. The general form of the **if** statement is

```
if(condition) {
  statement block 1
}
else {
  statement block 2
}
```

If single statements are used, the braces are not needed. The **else** is optional.

The *condition* may be any expression. If that expression evaluates to any value other than 0, then *statement block 1* will be executed; otherwise, if it exists, *statement block 2* will be executed.

The following fragment checks for the letter q, which terminates the program.

```
ch = cin.get();
if(ch == 'q') {
  cout << "program terminated";
  exit(0);
}
else proceed();
```

inline

The **inline** specifier tells the compiler to expand a function's code inline rather than calling the function. The **inline** specifier is a request, not a command, because several factors may prevent a function's code from being expanded inline. Some common restrictions include recursive functions, functions that contain loops or **switch** statements, or functions that contain static data. The **inline** specifier precedes the rest of a function's declaration. For example, the following tells the compiler to generate inline code for **myfunc()**:

```
inline void myfunc(int )
{
  // ...
}
```

When a function's definition is included within a class declaration, that function's code is automatically made inline, if possible.

int

int is the type specifier used to declare integer variables.

interrupt

The **interrupt** type specifier is not part of standard C++. It is used to declare functions that will be used as interrupt service routines.

long

long is a data type modifier used to declare double-length integer variables.

near

The **near** type modifier is not part of standard C++. It is used by compilers designed for use on the 8086 family of processors to force a pointer variable to use 16-bit, rather than 32-bit, addressing.

new

The **new** operator allocates dynamic memory and returns a pointer of the appropriate type to it. Its general form is shown here:

p_var = new *type*;

Here, *p_var* is a pointer variable that will receive the address of the allocated memory, and *type* is the type of data that the memory will hold. The **new** operator automatically allocates sufficient memory to hold one item of data of the specified type. For example, this code fragment allocates sufficient memory to hold a **double**:

```
double *p;

p = new double;
```

If the allocation request fails, **new** returns a null pointer.

You can initialize the allocated memory by specifying an initializer, using this general form:

p_var = new *type* (*initializer*);

Here, *initializer* is the value that will be assigned to the allocated memory.

To allocate a single-dimension array, use the following general form:

p_var = new *type*[*size*];

Here, *size* specifies the length of the array. **new** will automatically allocate sufficient room to hold an array of the specified type and of the specified size. When allocating arrays, no initializations may be given.

Multidimensional arrays may also be allocated using this general form:

p_var = new *type*[*size1*][*size2*]...[*sizeN*];

operator

The **operator** keyword is used to create overloaded operator functions. Operator functions come in two varieties: member and nonmember. The general form of a member operator function is shown here:

```
ret-type class-name::operator#(param-list) {
  // ...
}
```

Here, *ret-type* is the return type of the function, *class-name* is the name of the class relative to which the operator is overloaded, and *#* is the operator to be overloaded. When overloading a unary operator, the *param-list* is empty. (The operand is passed implicitly in **this**.) When overloading a binary operator, the *param-list* specifies the operand on the right side of the operator. (The operand on the left is passed implicitly in **this**.)

For nonmember functions, an operator function has this general form:

```
ret-type operator#(param-list) {
  // ...
}
```

Here, *param-list* contains one parameter when overloading a unary operator and two parameters when overloading a binary operator. When overloading a binary operator, the operand on the left is passed in the first parameter, and the operand on the right is passed in the right parameter.

Several restrictions apply to operator overloading. First, you may not alter the precedence of the operator. You may not change the number of operands required by an operator. You may not overload the following operators:

.   :   .*   ?

pascal

The **pascal** keyword is not defined by standard C++. It is used to force the compiler to compile a function in such a way that its parameter-passing convention is compatible with Pascal rather than C/C++.

private

The **private** access specifier is used to declare private elements of a class and to inherit a base class privately. When used to declare private elements of a class, it has this general form:

class *tag* {
 // ...
private: // make private
 // private elements
};

Members of a class are private by default. Thus, the access specifier **private** will be used in a class declaration to begin another block of private declarations. For example, this is a valid class declaration:

```
class myclass {
  int a, b; // private by default
public: begin public declarations
  int x, y; // these are public
private: // return to private declarations
  int c, d; // these are private
};
```

When used as an inheritance specifier, **private** has this general form:

class *tag* : private *base-class* { // ...

By specifying a base class as **private**, all public and protected members of the base class become private members of the derived class. All private members of the base class remain private to it.

protected

The **protected** access specifier is used to declare elements in a class that are private to that class but may be inherited by any derived class. It has the following general form:

```
class tag {
  // ...
protected: // make protected
  // protected elements
};
```

For example,

```
class base {
  // ...
protected:
  int a;
  // ...
};

// now, inherit base into derived class
class derived : public base {
  // ...
public:
  // ...
```

```
voidf() { cout << a; }
// derived has access to a
};
```

Here, **a** is private to **base** and may not be accessed by
any nonmember function. However, **derived** inherits
access to **a**. If **a** were simply defined as **private**, **derived**
would not have access to it.

public

The **public** access specifier is used to declare public
elements of a class and to publicly inherit a base class.
When used to declare public elements of a class, it has
this general form:

class *tag* {
  // private elements
public: // make public
  // public elements
};

Note   Members of a class are private by default. To
declare public elements of a class, you must specify
them as **public.**

When used as an inheritance specifier, **public** has this
general form:

class *tag* : public *base-class* { // ...

By specifying a base class as **public**, all public members
of the base class become public members of the derived
class, and all protected members of the base class
become protected members of the derived class. In all

cases, **private** members of the base class remain private to that base.

register

register is a storage class modifier used to request that access to a variable be optimized for speed. Traditionally used only on integer or character variables, **register** causes these variables to be stored in a register of the CPU instead of being placed in memory. However, the ANSI C standard broadened its definition to include all types of data. C++ follows the lead of the ANSI standard and allows **register** to be used on any type of data. However, data other than integers and characters cannot usually be stored in a CPU register. For other types of data, either cache memory (or some other sort of optimizing scheme) is used, or the **register** request is ignored.

register can only be used on local variables. In C, you cannot take the address of a **register** variable. However, in C++, you can (although doing so may prevent the variable from being optimized).

return

The **return** statement forces a return from a function and can be used to transfer a value back to the calling routine.

For example, the following function returns the product of its two integer arguments:

```
mul(int a, int b)
{
  return(a*b);
}
```

Keep in mind that as soon as a **return** is encountered, the function will return, skipping any other code that may be in the function.

Also, a function can contain more than one **return** statement.

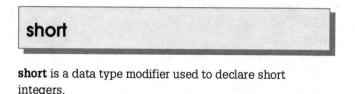

short

short is a data type modifier used to declare short integers.

signed

The **signed** type modifier is used to specify a **signed char** data type.

sizeof

The **sizeof** compile-time operator returns the length of the variable or type it precedes. If it precedes a type, that type must be enclosed in parentheses. If it precedes a variable, the parentheses are optional. For example, given the statements

```
int i;
cout << sizeof(int);
cout << sizeof i;
```

both output statements will print "2" for most PC-based
C++ compilers.

static

static is a data type modifier used to instruct the
compiler to create permanent storage for the local
variable that it precedes. This enables the specified
variable to maintain its value between function calls.

struct

The **struct** keyword is used to create an aggregate data
type called a structure, which may contain variables
and/or functions. In C++, a structure has the same
capabilities as a class except that by default, its
elements are public rather than private. A structure
declaration creates a class type. The general form of a
structure is

struct *tag* {
  // public members by default
  type pub1;
  type pub2;
  // ...
protected:
  // private members that may be inherited
  type prot1;
  type prot2;

```
  // ...
private:
  // private members
  type priv1;
  type priv2;
  // ...
} object-list;
```

The *tag* is the type name of the structure, which is a class type. The individual elements are referenced using the dot when operating on a structure or by using the arrow operator when operating through a pointer to the structure. The *object-list* is optional.

For example, the following structure contains a string called **name** and two integers called **high** and **low**. It also declares one variable called **my_var**.

```
struct my_struct {
  char name[80];
  int high;
  int low;
} my_var;
```

The section entitled "Data Types and Variables" covers this in more detail.

switch

The **switch** statement is C++'s multiway branch statement. It is used to route execution one of several different ways. The general form of the statement is

```
switch (control_var) {
  case constant 1: statement sequence 1;
    break;
```

```
case constant 2: statement sequence 2;
  break;
  .

  .

  .

case constant n: statement sequence n;
    break;
  default: default statements;
}
```

Each statement sequence may be from one to several statements long. The **default** portion is optional.

The **switch** works by checking the control_var against the constants. If a match is found, that sequence of statements is executed. If the statement sequence associated with the **case** that matches the value of control_var does not contain a **break**, execution will continue on into the next **case**. Put differently, from the point of the match, execution will continue until either a **break** statement is found or the **switch** ends. If no match is found and a **default** case is existent, its statement sequence is executed. Otherwise, no action takes place. The following example processes a menu selection:

```
ch = cin.get();

switch (ch) {
  case 'e': enter();
    break;
  case 'l': list();
    break;
  case 's': sort();
    break;
  case 'q': exit(0);
  default: cout << "unknown command\n";
    cout << "try again\n";
}
```

template

The **template** keyword is used to create generic functions and classes. In a generic function or class, the type of data that is used is specified as a parameter. Thus one function or class definition can be used with several different types of data.

A generic function defines a general set of operations that will be applied to various types of data. A generic function has the type of data that it will operate upon passed to it as a parameter. Using this mechanism, the same general procedure can be applied to a wide range of data. As you know, many algorithms are logically the same no matter what type of data is being operated upon. For example, the Quicksort algorithm is the same whether it is applied to an array of integers or an array of floating point numbers. It is just that the type of the data being sorted is different. By creating a generic function, you can define, independent of any data, the nature of the algorithm. Once this is done, the compiler automatically generates the correct code for the type of data that is actually used when you execute the function. In essence, when you create a generic function you are creating a function that can automatically overload itself.

The general form of a **template** function definition is shown here:

```
template <class data-type>
type func-name(parameter list)
{
  // body of function
}
```

Here, *data-type* is a placeholder for the type of data upon which the function will actually operate. It is important to understand that no other statements may occur between the **template** statement and the start of the generic function definition.

Here is an example. The following program creates a generic function that swaps the values of the two variables it is called with. Because the general process of exchanging two values is independent of the type of the variables, it is a good candidate to be made into a generic function.

```cpp
// Function template example.
#include <iostream.h>

template <class X> // template
void swap(X &a, X &b)
{
  X temp;

  temp = a;
  a = b;
  b = temp;
}

main()
{
  int i=10, j=20;
  float x=10.1, y=23.3;

  cout << "Original i, j: " << i << ' ' << j
       << endl;
  cout << "Original x, y: " << x << ' ' << y
       << endl;

  swap(i, j); // swap integers
  swap(x, y); // swap floats
```

```
cout << "Swapped i, j: " << i << ' ' << j
     << endl;
cout << "Swapped x, y: " << x << ' ' << y
     << endl;

return 0;
}
```

In this program, the line,

```
template <class X>
```

tells the compiler two things. First, that a template class is being created and second, that a generic definition is beginning. Here, **X** is a generic type that is used as a placeholder. After the **template** statement, the function **swap()** is declared, using **X** as the data type of the values that will be swapped. In **main()**, the **swap()** function is called using two different types of data: integers and floating point numbers. Because **swap()** is a generic function, the compiler automatically creates two versions of **swap()**—one that will exchange integer values and one that will exchange floating point values.

Remember   When you create a generic function, you are, in essence, allowing the compiler to generate as many different versions of that function as are necessary to handle the various ways that your program calls that function.

You may define more than one generic type using the **template** statement, with a comma-separated list. Generic functions are similar to overloaded functions except that they are more restrictive. When functions are overloaded, you may have different actions performed within the body of each function. A generic function must perform the same general action for all versions.

In addition to generic functions, you may also define a *generic class*. When you do this, you create a class that defines all algorithms used by that class, but the actual type of the data being manipulated will be specified as a parameter when objects of that class are created.

Generic classes are useful when a class contains generalizable logic. For example, the same algorithm that maintains a queue of integers will also work for a queue of characters. Also, the same mechanism that maintains a linked list of mailing addresses will also maintain a linked list of auto parts. By using a generic class, you can create a class that will maintain a queue, linked list, and so on for any type of data. The compiler will automatically generate the correct type of object based upon the type you specify when the object is created.

Here is the general form of a generic class declaration:

```
template <class data_type>
class class-name {
  // ...
};
```

In this case, *data_type* is a placeholder for a type of data that the class will operate on. When you declare an object of a generic class, you specify the type of data between angle brackets, using this general form:

class-name<*type*> *object*;

The following is an example of a generic class. This program creates a very simple generic singly linked list class. It then demonstrates the class by creating a linked list that stores characters.

```
// A simple generic linked list.
#include <iostream.h>
```

```
template <class data_t>
class list {
  data_t data;
  list *next;
public:
  list(data_t d);
  void add(list *node) {node->next = this;
                        next = 0; }
  list *getnext() { return next; }
  data_t getdata() { return data; }
};

template <class data_t>
list<data_t>::list(data_t d)
{
  data = d;
  next = 0;
}


main()
{
  list<char> start('a');
  list<char> *p, *last;
  int i;

  // build a list
  last = &start;
  for(i=0; i<26; i++) {
    p = new list<char> ('a' + i);
    p->add(last);
    last = p;
  }

  // follow the list
  p = &start;
  while(p) {
    cout << p->getdata();
    p = p->getnext();
  }
```

```
    return 0;
}
```

As you can see, the declaration of a generic class is
similar to that of a generic function. Notice, however,
how a function defined outside the class is handled. The
actual type of data stored by the list is made generic in
the class declaration. In **main()**, objects and pointers are
created that specify that the data type of the list will
be **char**.

Pay special attention to this declaration:

```
list<char> start('a');
```

Notice how the desired data type is passed inside the
angle brackets.

this

this is a pointer to the object that generated a call to a
member function. All member functions are
automatically passed a **this** pointer.

throw

throw is experimental. It is used to transfer control to an
exception handler. The exception is "caught" by **catch**.

Consult your user manual for details.

try is experimental and is part of C++'s exception-handling mechanism.

Consult your user manual for details.

The **typedef** keyword allows you to create a new name for an existing data type. The data type may be either one of the built-in types, or a class, structure, union, or enumeration. The general form of **typedef** is

typedef *type_specifier new_name*;

For example, to use the word **balance** in place of **float**, you would write

```
typedef float balance;
```

union

A union is a special type of class that assigns two or more variables to the same memory location. The form of the definition and the way the . (dot) and –> (arrow) operators reference an element are the same as for a class. By default, its elements are public. The general form is

union *tag* {
 // public members by default
 type pub1;

```
   type pub2;
   // ....
private:
  // private members
  type priv1;
  type priv2;
} object-list;
```

The *tag* is the type name for the union. For example, this creates a union between a **double** and a character string and creates one variable called **my_var**.

```
union my_union {
   char time[30];
   double offset;
} my_var;
```

This is covered in more detail in the section "Data Types and Variables."

unsigned

unsigned is a data type modifier that tells the compiler to eliminate the sign bit of an integer and to use all bits for arithmetic. This has the effect of doubling the size of the largest integer, but restricts it to only positive numbers.

virtual

The **virtual** function specifier creates a *virtual function*. A virtual function is a member of a base class that may be overridden by a derived class. If the function is not overridden by a derived class, the base class's definition is used.

A *pure virtual function* is a member function that has no definition. This means that a pure virtual function *must be* overridden in a derived class. A pure virtual function is prototyped like this:

virtual *ret-type* fname(*param-list*) = 0;

Here, *ret-type* is the return type of the function, *fname* is the function's name, and *param-list* specifies any parameters. The important feature is the **= 0.** This tells the compiler that the virtual function has no definition relative to the base class.

Run-time polymorphism is attained when virtual functions are accessed through a base class pointer. When this is done, the type of object pointed to determines which version of the virtual function is called.

void

The **void** type specifier is primarily used to explicitly declare functions that return no value. It is also used to create **void** pointers (pointers to **void**), which are generic pointers that are capable of pointing to any type of object.

volatile

The **volatile** modifier is used to tell the compiler that a variable may have its contents altered in ways not explicitly defined by the program. For example, variables that are changed by hardware such as real-time clocks, interrupts, or other inputs should be declared as **volatile**.

while

The **while** loop has the general form

```
while(condition) {
 statement block
}
```

If a single statement is the object of the **while**, then the braces may be omitted.

The **while** tests its *condition* at the top of the loop. Therefore, if the *condition* is false to begin with, the loop will not execute even once. The *condition* may be any expression.

The following is an example of a **while**, loop. It will read 100 characters and store them into a character array.

```
char s[256];

t = 0;

while(t<100) {
  s[t] = stream.get();
  t++;
}
```

The C++ Preprocessor

C++ includes several preprocessor directives, which are used to give instructions to the compiler. The preprocessor directives are listed here:

#define
#elif
#else
#endif
#error
#if
#ifdef
#ifndef
#include
#line
#pragma
#undef

Each is discussed briefly in this section.

#define

#define is used to perform macro substitutions of one piece of text for another throughout the file in which it is used. The general form of the directive is

#define *name character-sequence*

Here, each time *name* is encountered the specified *character-sequence* is substituted. Notice that there is no semicolon in this statement. Further, once the character sequence has started, it is terminated only by the end of the line.

For example, if you wish to use the value 1 for the word "TRUE" and the value 0 for the word "FALSE", you would declare these two macro **#define** statements:

```
#define TRUE 1
#define FALSE 0
```

This will cause the compiler to substitute a 1 or a 0 each time the word TRUE or FALSE is encountered.

The **#define** directive has another feature: the macro can have arguments. A macro that takes arguments acts much like a function. In fact, this type of macro is often referred to as a *function-like macro*. Each time the macro is encountered, the arguments associated with it are replaced by the actual arguments found in the program. For example,

```
#include <iostream.h>

#define ABS(a)   (a)<0 ? -(a) : (a)

main()
{
  cout << "abs of -1 and 1: " << ABS(-1)
          << ' ' << ABS(1);

  return 0;
}
```

When this program is compiled, **a** in the macro definition will be substituted with the values −1 and 1.

The parentheses surrounding **a** are necessary to ensure proper substitution in all cases. For example, if the parentheses around **a** were removed, this expression

```
ABS(10-20)
```

would be converted to

```
10-20<0 ? -10-20 : 10-20
```

thus yielding the wrong result.

Note   Because C++ supports the inlining of functions via
the **inline** specifier (which automatically eliminates the
problem just described), most C++ programmers no longer
use function-like macros. However, for compatibility with
C, the function-like macro is still allowed.

#error

The **#error** directive forces the compiler to stop
compilation when it is encountered. It is used primarily
for debugging. Its general form is

#error *message*

When **#error** is encountered, the message and the line
number are displayed.

#if, #ifdef, #ifndef, #else, #elif, and #endif

These preprocessor directives are used to selectively
compile various portions of a program. The general idea
is that if the expression after an **#if**, **#ifdef**, or **#ifndef** is
true, the code that is between one of the preceding and
an **#endif** will be compiled; otherwise it will be skipped
over. The **#endif** is used to mark the end of an **#if** block.
The **#else** can be used with any of the above in a
manner similar to the **else** in the C++ **if** statement.

The general form of **#if** is

#if *constant-expression*

If the constant expression is true, the block of code that immediately follows will be compiled.

The general form of **#ifdef** is

#ifdef *macro-name*

If the *macro-name* has been defined in a **#define** statement, the following block of code will be compiled.

The general form of **#ifndef** is

#ifndef *macro-name*

If *macro-name* is currently undefined by a **#define** statement, the block of code is compiled.

For example, here is the way some of these preprocessor directives work together. The following code

```
#include <iostream.h>

#define ted 10

main()
{
#ifdef ted
  cout << "Hi Ted\n";
#endif
  cout << "bye bye\n";
#if 10<9
  cout << "Hi George\n";
#endif

  return 0;
}
```

will print "Hi Ted" and "bye bye" on the screen, but not "Hi George".

The **#elif** directive is used to create an **if-else-if** statement. Its general form is

#elif *constant-expression*

The **#elif** may be used with the **#if** but not the **#ifdef** or **#ifndef** directives.

You can also use **#if** or **#elif** to determine if a macro name is defined using the **defined** preprocessing operator. It takes this general form:

#if defined *macro-name*
statement sequence
#endif

If the *macro-name* is defined, the statement sequence will be compiled. Otherwise it will be skipped. For example, the following program compiles the conditional code because **DEBUG** is defined by the program.

```
#include <iostream.h>

#define DEBUG

main()
{
  int i=100;
/* ... */
#if defined DEBUG
  cout << "value of i is: " << i << endl;
#endif
/*...*/
}
```

You can also precede **defined** with the ! operator to cause conditional compilation when the macro is not defined.

#include

The **#include** preprocessor directive instructs the compiler to read and compile another source file. It takes these general forms:

#include "*filename*"

#include <*filename*>

The source file to be read in must be enclosed between double quotes or angle brackets. For example,

```
#include <iostream.h>
```

will instruct the compiler to read and compile the header for the C++ I/O routines.

If the filename is enclosed by angle brackets, the file is searched for in a manner defined by the creator of the compiler. Often, this means searching some special directory set aside for **include** files. If the filename is enclosed in quotes, the file is looked for in another implementation-defined manner. For many implementations, this means searching the current working directory. If the file is not found, the search is repeated as if the filename had been enclosed in angle brackets. You must check your compiler's user manual for details on the differences between angle brackets and double quotes.

#include statements may be nested within other included files.

#line

The **#line** directive is used to change the contents of
_ _LINE_ _ and _ _FILE_ _, which are predefined
identifiers in the compiler. The basic form of the
command is

#line *number* "*filename*"

where *number* is any positive integer and the *filename*
is any valid file identifier. The value of *number* becomes
the number of the current source line and *filename*
becomes the name of the source file. The name of the
file is optional. **#line** is primarily used for debugging
purposes and special applications.

The _ _LINE_ _ identifier is an integer, and _ _FILE_ _ is
a null-terminated string.

For example, the following sets the current line counter
to 10 and the filename to "test".

```
#line 10 "test"
```

#pragma

The **#pragma** directive is an implementation-defined
directive that allows various instructions to be given to
the compiler. For example, a compiler may have an
option to support the tracing of program execution. A
trace option would then be specified by a **#pragma**
statement. You must check the user manual of the
compiler for details and options.

#undef

The **#undef** directive is used to remove a previously defined macro name. The general form is

#undef *macro-name*

For example, in the following code,

```
#define LEN 100
#define WIDTH 100

char array[LEN][WIDTH];

#undef LEN
#undef WIDTH
/* at this point both LEN and WIDTH are
   undefined */
```

both **LEN** and **WIDTH** are defined until the **#undef** statements are encountered.

The # and ## Preprocessor Operators

C++ provides two preprocessor operators: # and ##. These operators are used when in a **#define** macro.

The # operator causes the argument it precedes to be turned into a quoted string. For example, consider this program:

```
#include <iostream.h>

#define mkstr(s)   # s
```

```
main()
{
   cout << mkstr(I like C++);

   return 0;
}
```

The preprocessor turns the line

```
cout << mkstr(I like C++);
```

into

```
cout << "I like C++";
```

The ## operator is used to concatenate two tokens. For example, in the following program,

```
#include <iostream.h>

#define concat(a, b)   a ## b

main()
{
   int xy = 10;

   cout << concat(x, y);

   return 0;
}
```

the preprocessor transforms

```
cout << concat(x, y);
```

into

```
cout << xy;
```

If these operators seem strange to you, keep in mind that they are not needed or used in most C++ programs.

They exist primarily to allow some special cases to be handled by the preprocessor.

Predefined Macro Names

C++ specifies five built-in predefined macro names. They are

_ _**LINE**_ _
_ _**FILE**_ _
_ _**DATE**_ _
_ _**TIME**_ _
_ _**cplusplus**

The _ _**LINE**_ _ and _ _**FILE**_ _ macros are discussed in the **#line** discussion. The others will be examined here.

The _ _**DATE**_ _ macro is a string, in the form *month/day/year,* that is the date of the translation of the source file into object code.

The time of the translation of the source code into object code is contained as a string in _ _**TIME**_ _. The form of the string is *hour:minute:second.*

The macro _ _**cplusplus** is defined when compiling a C++ program.

It is also possible that your C++ compiler will define _ _**STDC**_ _. Check your user manual for details.

The Standard I/O Functions

This section details C++ I/O functions that are not object oriented. These functions are defined by the ANSI C standard, and all C++ compilers supply these functions in their standard libraries. They are supported by C++ to provide compatibility when migrating C code. However, there is no fundamental reason that you cannot use them in your C++ program when you deem it appropriate. Because the functions in this chapter are specified by the ANSI standard, they will be referred to collectively as the *ANSI I/O system*.

Note C++ also defines a set of object-oriented I/O functions, which are discussed in the section entitled "The C++ Class-Based I/O System." When writing object-oriented programs, you will most likely want to use the object-oriented I/O system instead of the ANSI I/O system described here.

The header file associated with the standard I/O functions is called STDIO.H. It defines several macros and types used by the file system. The most important type is **FILE**, which is used to declare a file pointer. Two other types are **size_t** and **fpos_t**, which are essentially equivalent to **unsigned**. The **size_t** type defines an object that is capable of holding the size of the largest file allowed by the operating environment. The **fpos_t** type defines an object that can hold all information needed to uniquely specify every position within a file.

The ANSI I/O system operates through *streams*. A stream is a logical device that is connected to an actual physical device, which is referred to as the *file* when a file is opened.

In the ANSI I/O system, all streams have the same capabilities, but files may have differing qualities. For example, a disk file allows random access, but a modem does not. Thus, the ANSI I/O system provides a level of abstraction between the programmer and the physical device. The abstraction is the stream and the device is the file. In this way, a consistent logical interface can be maintained, even though the actual physical devices may differ.

A stream is connected to a file via a call to **fopen()**. Streams are operated upon through the file pointer (which is a pointer of type **FILE ***). In a sense, the file pointer is the glue that holds the system together.

When your program begins execution, three predefined streams are automatically opened. They are **stdin**, **stdout**, and **stderr**, referring to standard input, standard output, and standard error, respectively. By default, these are connected to the console, but they may be redirected to any other type of device.

Many of the standard library I/O functions set the built-in global integer variable **errno** when an error occurs. Your program can check this variable when an error occurs to obtain more information about the error. The values that **errno** may take are implementation dependent.

clearerr

```
#include <stdio.h>
void clearerr(FILE *stream);
```

The **clearerr()** function resets the file error flag pointed to by *stream* to 0 (off). The end-of-file indicator is also reset.

The error flags for each stream are initially set to 0 by a successful call to **fopen()**. Once an error has occurred, the flags stay set until either an explicit call to **clearerr()** or **rewind()** is made.

File errors can occur for a wide variety of reasons, many of which are system dependent. The exact nature of the error can be determined by calling **perror()**, which displays what error has occurred (see **perror**).

Related functions are **feof()**, **ferror()**, and **perror()**.

fclose

```
#include <stdio.h>
int fclose(FILE *stream);
```

The **fclose()** function closes the file associated with *stream* and flushes its buffer. After an **fclose()**, *stream* is no longer connected with the file, and any automatically allocated buffers are deallocated.

If **fclose()** is successful, 0 is returned; otherwise a nonzero value is returned. Trying to close a file that has already been closed is an error. Removing the storage media before closing a file will also generate an error, as will lack of sufficient free disk space.

Related functions are **fopen()**, **freopen()**, and **fflush()**.

feof

```
#include <stdio.h>
int feof(FILE *stream);
```

The **feof()** function checks the file position indicator to determine if the end of the file associated with *stream* has been reached. A nonzero value is returned if the file position indicator is at end-of-file; 0 is returned otherwise.

Once the end of the file has been reached, subsequent read operations will return **EOF** until either **rewind()** is called or the file position indicator is moved using **fseek()**. The macro **EOF** is defined in STDIO.H.

The **feof()** function is particularly useful when working with binary files because the end-of-file marker is also a valid binary integer. Explicit calls must be made to **feof()** rather than simply testing the return value of **getc()**, for example, to determine when the end of a binary file has been reached.

Related functions are **clearerr()**, **ferror()**, **perror()**, **putc()**, and **getc()**.

ferror

```
#include <stdio.h>
int ferror(FILE *stream);
```

The **ferror()** function checks for a file error on the given *stream*. A return value of 0 indicates that no error has occurred, while a nonzero value means an error.

The error flags associated with *stream* will stay set until either the file is closed, or **rewind()** or **clearerr()** is called.

To determine the exact nature of the error, use the **perror()** function.

Related functions are **clearerr()**, **feof()**, and **perror()**.

fflush

```
#include <stdio.h>
int fflush(FILE *stream);
```

If *stream* is associated with a file opened for writing, a call to **fflush()** causes the contents of the output buffer to be physically written to the file. If *stream* points to an input file, the contents of the input buffer are cleared. In either case, the file remains open.

A return value of 0 indicates success; **EOF** indicates that a write error has occurred.

All buffers are automatically flushed upon normal termination of the program or when they are full. Also, closing a file flushes its buffer.

Related functions are **fclose()**, **fopen()**, **fread()**, **fwrite()**, **getc()**, and **putc()**.

fgetc

```
#include <stdio.h>
int fgetc(FILE *stream);
```

The **fgetc()** function returns the next character from the input *stream* from the current position and increments the file position indicator. The character is read as an **unsigned char** that is converted to an integer.

If the end of the file is reached, **fgetc()** returns **EOF**. However, since **EOF** is a valid integer value, when working with binary files you must use **feof()** to check for the end of the file. If **fgetc()** encounters an error, **EOF** is also returned. Again, if working with binary files, you must use **ferror()** to check for file errors.

Related functions are **fputc()**, **getc()**, **putc()**, and **fopen()**.

fgetpos

```
#include <stdio.h>
int fgetpos(FILE *stream, fpos_t *position);
```

The **fgetpos()** function stores the current value of the file position indicator in the object pointed to by *position*. The object pointed to by *position* must be of type **fpos_t**, which is a type defined in STDIO.H. The value stored there is useful only in a subsequent call to **fsetpos()**.

If an error occurs, **fgetpos()** returns nonzero; otherwise it returns 0.

Related functions are **fsetpos()**, **fseek()**, and **ftell()**.

fgets

```
#include <stdio.h>
char *fgets(char *str, int num, FILE *stream);
```

The **fgets()** function reads up to *num–1* characters from *stream* and places them into the character array pointed to by *str*. Characters are read until either a newline or an **EOF** is received or until the specified limit is reached. After the characters have been read, a null is placed in the array immediately after the last character read. A newline character will be retained and will be part of *str*.

If successful, **fgets()** returns *str*; a null pointer is returned upon failure. If a read error occurs the contents of the array pointed to by *str* are indeterminate. Because a null pointer will be returned when either an error has occurred or when the end of the file is reached, you should use **feof()** or **ferror()** to determine what has actually happened.

Related functions are **fputs()**, **fgetc()**, **gets()**, and **puts()**.

fopen

```
#include <stdio.h>
FILE *fopen(const char *fname, const char *mode);
```

The **fopen()** function opens a file whose name is pointed to by *fname* and returns the stream that is associated with it. The type of operations that will be allowed on the file are defined by the value of *mode*. The legal values for *mode* are shown in the following table. The filename must be a string of characters comprising a valid filename as defined by the operating system and may include a path specification if the environment supports it.

Mode	Meaning
"r"	Open text file for reading
"w"	Create a text file for writing
"a"	Append to text file
"rb"	Open binary file for reading

Mode	Meaning
"wb"	Create binary file for writing
"ab"	Append to a binary file
"r+"	Open text file for read/write
"w+"	Create text file for read/write
"a+"	Open text file for read/write
"rb+"	Open binary file for read/write
"wb+"	Create binary file for read/write
"ab+"	Open binary file for read/write

If **fopen()** is successful in opening the specified file, a **FILE** pointer is returned. If the file cannot be opened, a null pointer is returned.

As the table shows, a file may be opened in either text or binary mode. In text mode, some character translations may occur. For example, newlines may be converted into carriage return/linefeed sequences. No such translations occur on binary files.

The correct method of opening a file is illustrated by this code fragment:

```
FILE *fp;

if ((fp = fopen("test", "w"))==NULL) {
  cout << "cannot open file\n";
  exit(1);
}
```

This method detects any error in opening a file, such as a write-protected or a full disk, before attempting to write to it. A null is used to indicate an error because no file pointer will ever have that value. **NULL** is defined in STDIO.H.

If you use **fopen()** to open a file for output, any preexisting file by that name will be erased and a new file started. If no file by that name exists, one will be created. If you want to add to the end of the file, you must use mode "a". If the file does not exist, an error will be returned. Opening a file for read operations requires that the file exists. If it does not exist, an error will be returned. Finally, if a file is opened for read/write operations, it will not be erased if it exists; however, if it does not exist it will be created.

When accessing a file opened for read/write operations, you may not follow an output operation with an input operation without an intervening call to either **fflush()**, **fseek()**, **fsetpos()**, or **rewind()**. Also, you may not follow an input operation with an output operation without an intervening call to one of the previously mentioned functions.

Related functions are **fclose()**, **fread()**, **fwrite()**, **putc()**, and **getc()**.

fprintf

```
#include <stdio.h>
int fprintf(FILE *stream, const char *format, ...);
```

The **fprintf()** function outputs the values of the arguments that comprise the argument list as specified in the *format* string to the stream pointed to by *stream*. The return value is the number of characters actually printed. If an error occurs, a negative number is returned.

There may be from zero to several arguments with the maximum number being system dependent.

The operations of the format control string and commands are identical to those in **printf()**; see **printf** for a complete description.

Related functions are **printf()** and **fscanf()**.

fputc

```
#include <stdio.h>
int fputc(int ch, FILE *stream);
```

The **fputc()** function writes the character *ch* to the specified stream at the current file position and then advances the file position indicator. Even though *ch* is declared to be an **int** for historical purposes, it is converted by **fputc()** into an **unsigned char**. Because all character arguments are elevated to integers at the time of the call, you will generally see character variables used as arguments. If an integer were used, the high-order byte would simply be discarded.

The value returned by **fputc()** is the value of the character written. If an error occurs, **EOF** is returned. For files opened for binary operations, an **EOF** may be a valid character, and the function **ferror()** will need to be used to determine whether an error has actually occurred.

Related functions are **fgetc()**, **fopen()**, **fprintf()**, **fread()**, and **fwrite()**.

fputs

```
#include <stdio.h>
int fputs(const char *str, FILE *stream);
```

The **fputs()** function writes the contents of the string pointed to by *str* to the specified stream. The null terminator is not written.

The **fputs()** function returns nonnegative on success and **EOF** on failure.

If the stream is opened in text mode, certain character translations may take place. This means that there may not be a one-to-one mapping of the string onto the file. However, if the stream is opened in binary mode, no character translations will occur, and a one-to-one mapping between the string and the file will exist.

Related functions are **fgets()**, **gets()**, **puts()**, **fprintf()**, and **fscanf()**.

fread

```
#include <stdio.h>
int fread(void *buf, size_t size, size_t
          count, FILE *stream);
```

The **fread()** function reads *count* number of objects, each object being *size* bytes in length, from the stream pointed to by *stream* and places them in the array pointed to by *buf*. The file position indicator is advanced by the number of characters read.

The **fread()** function returns the number of items actually read. If fewer items are read than are requested in the call, either an error has occurred or the end of the file has been reached. You must use **feof()** or **ferror()** to determine what has taken place.

If the stream is opened for text operations, certain character translations, such as carriage return/linefeed sequences being transformed into newlines, may occur.

Related functions are **fwrite()**, **fopen()**, **fscanf()**, **fgetc()**, and **getc()**.

freopen

```
#include <stdio.h>
FILE *freopen(const char *fname, const char
              *mode, FILE *stream);
```

The **freopen()** function associates an existing stream with a different file. The new file's name is pointed to by *fname*, the access mode is pointed to by *mode*, and the stream to be reassigned is pointed to by *stream*. The string *mode* uses the same format as **fopen()**; a complete discussion is found in the **fopen()** description.

When called, **freopen()** first tries to close a file that may currently be associated with *stream*. However, if the attempt to close the file fails, the **freopen()** function still continues to open the other file.

The **freopen()** function returns a pointer to *stream* on success and a null pointer otherwise.

The main use of **freopen()** is to redirect the system defined files **stdin**, **stdout**, and **stderr** to some other file.

Related functions are **fopen()** and **fclose()**.

fscanf

```
#include <stdio.h>
int fscanf(FILE *stream, const char *format, ...);
```

The **fscanf()** function works exactly like the **scanf()** function, except that it reads the information from the stream specified by *stream* instead of **stdin**. See **scanf** for details.

The **fscanf()** function returns the number of arguments actually assigned values. This number does not include skipped fields. A return value of **EOF** means that a failure occurred before the first assignment was made.

Related functions are **scanf()** and **fprintf()**.

fseek

```
#include <stdio.h>
int fseek(FILE *stream, long offset, int origin);
```

The **fseek()** function sets the file position indicator associated with *stream* according to the values of *offset* and *origin*. Its purpose is to support random I/O operations. The *offset* is the number of bytes from *origin* to seek to. The values for *origin* must be one of these macros (defined in STDIO.H):

Name	Meaning
SEEK_SET	Seek from start of file
SEEK_CUR	Seek from current location
SEEK_END	Seek from end of file

A return value of 0 means that **fseek()** succeeded. A nonzero value indicates failure.

You may use **fseek()** to move the position indicator anywhere in the file, even beyond the end. However, it is an error to attempt to set the position indicator before the beginning of the file.

The **fseek()** function clears the end-of-file flag associated with the specified stream. Furthermore, it nullifies any prior **ungetc()** on the same stream (see **ungetc**).

Related functions are **ftell()**, **rewind()**, **fopen()**, **fgetpos()**, and **fsetpos()**.

fsetpos

```
#include <stdio.h>
int fsetpos(FILE *stream, const fpos_t *position);
```

The **fsetpos()** function moves the file position indicator to the point specified by the object pointed to by *position*. This value must have been previously obtained through a call to **fgetpos()**. The type **fpos_t** is defined in STDIO.H. After **fsetpos()** is executed, the end-of-file indicator is reset. Also, any previous call to **ungetc()** is nullified.

If **fsetpos()** fails, it returns nonzero. If it is successful, it returns 0.

Related functions are **fgetpos()**, **fseek()**, and **ftell()**.

ftell

```
#include <stdio.h>
long ftell(FILE *stream);
```

The **ftell()** function returns the current value of the file position indicator for the specified stream. In the case of binary streams, the value is the number of bytes the indicator is from the beginning of the file. For text streams, the return value may not be meaningful except as an argument to **fseek()** because of possible character translations, such as carriage return/linefeeds being substituted for newlines, which affect the apparent size of the file.

The **ftell()** function returns –1L when an error occurs. If the stream is incapable of random seeks—if it is a modem, for instance—the return value is undefined.

Related functions are **fseek()** and **fgetpos()**.

fwrite

```
#include <stdio.h>
int fwrite(const void *buf, size_t
          size, size_t count, FILE *stream);
```

The **fwrite()** function writes *count* number of objects, each object being *size* bytes in length, to the stream pointed to by *stream* from the character array pointed to by *buf*. The file position indicator is advanced by the number of characters written.

The **fwrite()** function returns the number of items actually written which, if the function is successful, will equal the number requested. If fewer items are written than are requested, an error has occurred. For text streams, various character translations may take place but will have no effect upon the return value.

Related functions are **fread()**, **fscanf()**, **getc()**, and **fgetc()**.

getc

```
#include <stdio.h>
int getc(FILE *stream);
```

The **getc()** function returns the next character from the input *stream* from the current position and increments the file position indicator. The character is read as an **unsigned char** that is converted to an integer.

If the end of the file is reached, **getc()** returns **EOF**. However, since **EOF** is a valid integer value, when working with binary files you must use **feof()** to check for the end-of-file character. If **getc()** encounters an error, **EOF** is also returned. If working with binary files, you must use **ferror()** to check for file errors.

The functions **getc()** and **fgetc()** are identical, and in most implementations **getc()** is simply defined as the macro shown here.

```
#define getc(fp) fgetc(fp)
```

This causes the **fgetc()** function to be substituted for the **getc()** macro.

Related functions are **fputc()**, **fgetc()**, **putc()**, and **fopen()**.

getchar

```
#include <stdio.h>
int getchar(void);
```

The **getchar()** function returns the next character from **stdin**. The character is read as an **unsigned char** that is converted to an integer.

If the end of the file is reached, **getchar()** returns **EOF**. However, since **EOF** is a valid integer value, when working with binary files you must use **feof()** to check for end-of-file. If **getchar()** encounters an error, **EOF** is also returned. If working with binary files, you must use **ferror()** to check for file errors.

The **getchar()** function is often implemented as a macro like this:

```
getchar(stdin)
```

Related functions are **fputc()**, **fgetc()**, **putc()**, and **fopen()**.

gets

```
#include <stdio.h>
char *gets(char *str);
```

The **gets()** function reads characters from **stdin** and places them into the character array pointed to by *str*.

Characters are read until a newline or an **EOF** is
received. The newline character is not made part of the
string; instead, it is translated into a null to terminate
the string.

If successful, **gets()** returns *str*; a null pointer is returned
upon failure. If a read error occurs the contents of the
array pointed to by *str* are indeterminate. Because a null
pointer will be returned when either an error has
occurred or when the end of the file is reached, you
should use **feof()** or **ferror()** to determine what has
actually happened.

There is no limit to the number of characters that **gets()**
will read, and it is therefore your job to make sure that
the array pointed to by *str* will not be overrun.

Related functions are **fputs()**, **fgetc()**, **fgets()**, and **puts()**.

perror

```
#include <stdio.h>
void perror(const char *str);
```

The **perror()** function maps the value of the global
variable **errno** onto a string and writes that string to
stderr. If the value of *str* is not null, the string is written
first, followed by a colon, and then the
implementation-defined error message.

printf

```
#include <stdio.h>
int printf(const char *format, ...);
```

The **printf()** function writes to **stdout** the arguments
that comprise the argument list as specified by the
string pointed to by *format*.

The string pointed to by *format* consists of two types of
items. The first type is made up of characters that will
be printed on the screen. The second type contains
format commands that define the way the arguments
are displayed. A format command begins with a percent
sign and is followed by the format code. There must be
exactly the same number of arguments as there are
format commands, and the format commands and the
arguments are matched in order. For example, the
following **printf()** call displays "Hi c 10 there!".

```
printf("Hi %c %d %s", 'c', 10, "there!");
```

If there are insufficient arguments to match the format
commands, the output is undefined. If there are more
arguments than format commands, the remaining
arguments are discarded. The format commands are
shown here:

Code	Format
%c	Character
%d	Signed decimal integers
%i	Signed decimal integers
%e	Scientific notation (lowercase e)
%E	Scientific notation (uppercase E)
%f	Decimal floating point
%g	Uses %e or %f, whichever is shorter (if %e, uses lowercase e)
%G	Uses %E or %f, whichever is shorter (if %E, uses uppercase E)

Code	Format
%o	Unsigned octal
%s	String of characters
%u	Unsigned decimal integers
%x	Unsigned hexadecimal (lowercase letters)
%X	Unsigned hexadecimal (uppercase letters)
%p	Displays a pointer
%n	The associated argument shall be an integer pointer into which is placed the number of characters written so far.
%%	Prints a % sign

The **printf()** function returns the number of characters actually printed. A negative return value indicates that an error has taken place.

The format commands may have modifiers that specify the field width, the number of decimal places, and a left-justification flag. An integer placed between the % sign and the format command acts as a *minimum field-width specifier*. This pads the output with blanks or 0's to ensure that it is at least a certain minimum length. If the string or number is greater than that minimum, it will be printed in full, even if it overruns the minimum. The default padding is done with spaces. If you wish to pad with 0's, place a 0 before the field-width specifier. For example, **%05d** will pad a number of less than 5 digits with 0's so that its total length is 5.

To specify the number of decimal places printed for a floating point number, place a decimal point followed by the number of decimal places you wish to display after the field-width specifier. For example, **%10.4f** will display a number at least ten characters wide with four decimal places. When this is applied to strings or integers, the number following the period specifies the maximum field length. For example, **%5.7s** will display a string that will be at least five characters long and will not exceed seven. If the string is longer than the maximum field width, the characters will be truncated off the end.

By default, all output is *right justified*: if the field width is larger than the data printed, the data will be placed on the right edge of the field. You can force the information to be left justified by placing a minus sign directly after the %. For example, **%–10.2f** will left-justify a floating point number with two decimal places in a ten-character field.

There are two format command modifiers that allow **printf()** to display **short** and **long** integers. These modifiers may be applied to the **d**, **i**, **o**, **u**, and **x** type specifiers. The l modifier tells **printf()** that a **long** data type follows. For example, **%ld** means that a **long int** is to be displayed. The **h** modifier instructs **printf()** to display a **short int**. Therefore, **%hu** indicates that the data is of type **short unsigned int**.

The l modifier may also prefix the floating point commands of **e**, **f**, and **g** and indicates that a **double** follows. To output a **long double**, use the **%L** prefix.

The **%n** command causes the number of characters that have been written at the time the **%n** is encountered to be placed in an integer variable whose pointer is specified in the argument list. For example, this code fragment displays the number 14 after the line "this is a test":

```
int i;

printf("this is a test%n", &i);
printf("%d", i);
```

The # has a special meaning when used with some **printf()** format codes. Preceding a **g**, **f**, or **e** code with a # ensures that the decimal point will be present, even if there are no decimal digits. If you precede the **x** format code with a #, the hexadecimal number will be printed with a 0x prefix. If you precede the **o** format with a #, the octal value will be printed with a **0** prefix. The # cannot be applied to any other format specifiers.

The minimum field-width and precision specifiers may be provided by arguments to **printf()** instead of by constants. To accomplish this, use an * as a placeholder. When the format string is scanned, **printf()** will match each * to an argument in the order in which they occur.

Related functions are **scanf()** and **fprintf()**.

putc

```
#include <stdio.h>
int putc(int ch, FILE *stream);
```

The **putc()** function writes the character contained in the least significant byte of *ch* to the output stream pointed to by *stream*. Because character arguments are elevated to integer at the time of the call, you may use character variables as arguments to **putc()**.

The **putc()** function returns the character written on success or **EOF** if an error occurs. If the output stream has been opened in binary mode, **EOF** is a valid value for *ch*. This means that you must use **ferror()** to determine if an error has occurred.

When implemented as a macro, the **putc()** function is often replaced with **fputc()**, since **fputc()** is functionally equivalent to **putc()**.

Related functions are **fgetc()**, **fputc()**, **getchar()**, and **putchar()**.

putchar

```
#include <stdio.h>
int putchar(int ch);
```

The **putchar()** function writes the character contained in the least significant byte of *ch* to **stdout**. It is functionally equivalent to **putc(ch, stdout)**. Because character arguments are elevated to integer at the time of the call, you may use character variables as arguments to **putchar()**.

The **putchar()** function returns the character written on success or **EOF** if an error occurs. If the output stream has been opened in binary mode, **EOF** is a valid value for *ch*. This means that you must use **ferror()** to determine if an error has occurred.

A related function is **putc()**.

puts

```
#include <stdio.h>
int puts(char *str);
```

The **puts()** function writes the string pointed to by *str* to the standard output device. The null terminator is translated to a newline.

The **puts()** function returns a nonnegative value if successful and an **EOF** upon failure.

Related functions are **putc()**, **gets()**, and **printf()**.

remove

```
#include <stdio.h>
int remove(const char *fname);
```

The **remove()** function erases the file specified by *fname*. It returns 0 if the file was successfully deleted and nonzero if an error occurred.

A related function is **rename()**.

rename

```
#include <stdio.h>
int rename(const char *oldfname, const
          *newfname);
```

The **rename()** function changes the name of the file specified by *oldfname* to *newfname*. The *newfname* must not match any existing directory entry.

The **rename()** function returns 0 if successful and nonzero if an error has occurred.

A related function is **remove()**.

rewind

```
#include <stdio.h>
void rewind(FILE *stream);
```

The **rewind()** function moves the file position indicator to the start of the specified stream. It also clears the end-of-file and error flags associated with *stream*. It has no return value.

A related function is **fseek()**.

scanf

```
#include <stdio.h>
int scanf(const char *format, ...);
```

The **scanf()** function is a general-purpose input routine that reads the stream **stdin** and stores the information in the variables pointed to in its argument list. It can read all the built-in data types and automatically convert them into the proper internal format.

The control string pointed to by *format* consists of three classifications of characters:

- Format specifiers
- Whitespace characters
- Non-whitespace characters

The input format specifiers are preceded by a % sign and tell **scanf()** what type of data is to be read next. The **scanf()** codes are matched in order with the variables receiving the input in the argument list. For example, **%s** reads a string while **%d** reads an integer. These codes are listed in the following table.

Code	Meaning
%c	Reads a single character
%d	Reads a decimal integer
%i	Reads an integer
%e	Reads a floating point number
%f	Reads a floating point number
%g	Reads a floating point number
%o	Reads an octal number
%s	Reads a string
%x	Reads a hexadecimal number
%p	Reads a pointer
%n	Receives an integer value equal to the number of characters read so far
%u	Reads an unsigned integer
%[]	Scans for a set of characters

The format string is read left to right and the format codes are matched, in order, with the arguments that comprise the argument list.

A whitespace character in the format string causes **scanf()** to skip over one or more whitespace characters in the input stream. A whitespace character is either a space, a tab character, or a newline. In essence, one whitespace character in the control string will cause **scanf()** to read, but not store, any number (including zero) of whitespace characters up to the first non-whitespace character.

A non-whitespace character in the format string causes **scanf()** to read and discard a matching character. For example, **"%d,%d"** causes **scanf()** to first read an integer, then read and discard a comma, and finally read another integer. If the specified character is not found, **scanf()** will terminate.

All the variables used to receive values through **scanf()** must be passed by their addresses. This means that all arguments must be pointers to the variables used as arguments.

The input data items must be separated by spaces, tabs, or newlines. Punctuation such as commas, semicolons, and the like do not count as separators. This means that

```
scanf("%d%d", &r, &c);
```

will accept an input of **10 20** but fail with **10,20**.

An * placed after the % and before the format code will read data of the specified type but suppress its assignment. Thus, the following command

```
scanf("%d%*c%d", &x, &y);
```

given the input **"10/20"**, will place the value 10 into **x**, discard the divide sign, and give **y** the value 20.

The format commands can specify a maximum field-length modifier. This is an integer number placed between the % and the format command code that limits the number of characters read for any field. For example, if you wish to read no more than 20 characters into **address**, then you would write

```
scanf("%20s", address);
```

If the input stream were greater than 20 characters, a subsequent call to input would begin where this call left off. Input for a field may terminate before the maximum field length is reached if a white space is encountered. In this case, **scanf()** moves on to the next field.

Although spaces, tabs, and newlines are used as field separators, when reading a single character, these are read like any other character. For example, with an input stream of "x y",

```
scanf("%c%c%c", &a, &b, &c);
```

will return with the character x in **a**, a space in **b** and the character y in **c**.

Beware, any other characters in the control string—including spaces, tabs, and newlines—will be used to match and discard characters from the input stream. Any character that matches is discarded. For example, given the input stream "10t20",

```
scanf("%st%s", &x, &y);
```

will place 10 into **x** and 20 into **y**. The t is discarded because of the t in the control string.

Another feature of **scanf()** is called a *scanset*. A scanset defines a set of characters that may be read by **scanf()** and assigned to the corresponding character array. A scanset is defined by putting a string of the characters you want to scan for inside square brackets. The beginning square bracket must be prefixed by a percent sign. For example, this scanset tells **scanf()** to read only the characters A, B, and C:

```
%[ABC]
```

When a scanset is used, **scanf()** continues to read characters and put them into the corresponding character array until a character that is not in the scanset is encountered. The corresponding variable must be a pointer to a character array. Upon return from **scanf()**, the array will contain a null-terminated string comprised of the characters read.

You can specify an inverted set if the first character in the set is a ∧. When the ∧ is present, it instructs **scanf()** to accept any character that *is not* defined by the scanset.

You can specify a range using a hypen. For example, this tells **scanf()** to accept the characters A through Z.

```
%[A-Z]
```

One important point to remember is that the scanset is case sensitive. Therefore, if you want to scan for both upper- and lowercase letters they must be specified individually.

The **scanf()** function returns a number equal to the number of fields that were successfully assigned values. This number will not include fields that were read but not assigned because the * modifier was used to suppress the assignment. **EOF** is returned if an error occurs before the first field is assigned.

Related functions are **printf()** and **fscanf()**.

setbuf

```
#include <stdio.h>
void setbuf(FILE *stream, char *buf);
```

The **setbuf()** function is used to either specify the buffer the specified stream will use or, if called with *buf* set to null, to turn off buffering. If a programmer-defined buffer is to be specified, it must be **BUFSIZ** characters long. **BUFSIZ** is defined in STDIO.H.

The **setbuf()** function returns no value.

Related functions are **fopen()**, **fclose()**, and **setvbuf()**.

setvbuf

```
#include <stdio.h>
int setvbuf(FILE *stream, char *buf, int
          mode, size_t size;
```

The **setvbuf()** function allows the programmer to specify the buffer, its size, and its mode for the specified stream. The character array pointed to by *buf* is used as the *stream* buffer for I/O operations. The size of the buffer is set by *size* and *mode* determines how buffering will be handled. If *buf* is null, **setvbuf()** will allocate its own buffer.

The legal values of *mode* are **_IOFBF**, **_IONBF**, and **_IOLBF**. These are defined in STDIO.H. When *mode* is set to **_IOFBF**, full buffering will take place. If *mode* is **_IOLBF**, the stream will be line buffered, which means that the buffer will be flushed each time a newline character is written for output streams; for input streams, an input request reads all characters up to a newline. In either case, the buffer is also flushed when full. If mode is **_IONBF**, no buffering takes place.

The value of *size* must be greater than 0.

The **setvbuf()** function returns 0 on success, nonzero on failure.

A related function is **setbuf()**.

sprintf

```
#include <stdio.h>
int sprintf(char *buf, const char *format, ...);
```

The **sprintf()** function is identical to **printf()** except that the output is put into the array pointed to by *buf* instead of being written to the console. See **printf** for details.

The return value is equal to the number of characters actually placed into the array.

Related functions are **printf()** and **fsprintf()**.

sscanf

```
#include <stdio.h>
int sscanf(const char *buf, const char
        *format, ...);
```

The **sscanf()** function is identical to **scanf()** except that data is read from the array pointed to by *buf* rather than **stdin**. See **scanf** for details.

The return value is equal to the number of variables that were actually assigned values. This number does not include fields that were skipped through the use of the ***** format command modifier. A value of 0 means that no fields were assigned, and **EOF** indicates that an error occurred prior to the first assignment.

Related functions are **scanf()** and **fscanf()**.

tmpfile

```
#include <stdio.h>
FILE *tmpfile(void);
```

The **tmpfile()** function opens a temporary file for update and returns a pointer to the stream. The function automatically uses a unique filename to avoid conflicts with existing files.

The **tmpfile()** function returns a null pointer on failure; otherwise it returns a pointer to the stream.

The temporary file created by **tmpfile()** is automatically removed when the file is closed or when the program terminates.

A related function is **tmpnam()**.

tmpnam

```
#include <stdio.h>
char *tmpnam(char *name);
```

The **tmpnam()** function generates a unique filename and stores it in the array pointed to by *name*. The main purpose of **tmpnam()** is to generate a temporary filename that is different from any other file in the current disk directory.

The function may be called up to **TMP_MAX** times. **TMP_MAX** is defined in STDIO.H, and it will be at least 25. Each time **tmpnam()** is called, it will generate a new temporary filename.

A pointer to *string* is returned on success; otherwise a null pointer is returned.

A related function is **tmpfile()**.

ungetc

```
#include <stdio.h>
int ungetc(int ch, FILE *stream);
```

The **ungetc()** function returns the character specified by the low-order byte of *ch* to the input stream *stream*. This character will then be returned by the next read operation on *stream*. A call to **fflush()** or **fseek()** undoes an **ungetc()** operation and discards the character.

A one-character pushback is guaranteed; however, some implementations will accept more.

You may not unget an **EOF**.

A call to **ungetc()** clears the end-of-file flag associated with the specified stream. The value of the file position indicator for a text stream is undefined until all pushed-back characters are read, in which case it will be the same as it was prior to the first **ungetc()** call. For binary streams, each **ungetc()** call decrements the file position indicator.

The return value is equal to *ch* on success and **EOF** on failure.

A related function is **getc()**.

vprintf, vfprintf, and vsprintf

```
#include <stdarg.h>
#include <stdio.h>
int vprintf(char *format, va_list arg_ptr);
int vfprintf(FILE *stream, const char
            *format, va_list arg_ptr);
int vsprintf(char *buf, char *format,
            va_list arg_ptr);
```

The functions **vprintf()**, **vfprintf()**, and **vsprintf()** are
functionally equivalent to **printf()**, **fprintf()**, and **sprintf()**,
respectively, except that the argument list has been
replaced by a pointer to a list of arguments. This pointer
must be of type **va_list** and is defined in STDARG.H.

Related functions are **va_arg()**, **va_start()**, and **va_end()**.

String and Character Functions

The C++ standard library has a rich and varied set of string and character handling functions. In C++, a string is a null-terminated array of characters. In a standard implementation, the string functions require the header file STRING.H to provide their prototypes. The character functions use CTYPE.H as their header file.

Because C++ has no bounds checking on array operations, it is the programmer's responsibility to prevent an array overflow. Neglecting to do so may cause your program to crash.

In C++, a *printable character* is one that can be displayed on a termimal. These are usually the characters between a space (0x20) and tilde (0xFE). *Control characters* have values between (0) and (0x1F) as well as DEL (0x7F).

For historical reasons, the arguments to the character functions are integer. However, only the low-order byte is used; the character function automatically converts the argument to **unsigned char**. However, you are free to call these functions with character arguments because characters are automatically elevated to integers at the time of the call.

The header file STRING.H defines the **size_t** type, which is essentially the same as **unsigned**.

isalnum

```
#include <ctype.h>
int isalnum(int ch);
```

The **isalnum()** function returns nonzero if its argument is either a letter of the alphabet or a digit. If the character is not alphanumeric, 0 is returned.

Related functions are **isalpha()**, **iscntrl()**, **isdigit()**, **isgraph()**, **isprint()**, **ispunct()**, and **isspace()**.

isalpha

```
#include <ctype.h>
int isalpha(int ch);
```

The **isalpha()** function returns nonzero if *ch* is a letter of the alphabet; otherwise 0 is returned. What constitutes a letter of the alphabet may vary from language to language. For English, these are the upper- and lowercase letters A through Z.

Related functions are **isalnum()**, **iscntrl()**, **isdigit()**, **isgraph()**, **isprint()**, **ispunct()**, and **isspace()**.

iscntrl

```
#include <ctype.h>
int iscntrl(int ch);
```

The **iscntrl()** function returns nonzero if *ch* is between 0 and 0x1F or is equal to 0x7F (DEL); otherwise 0 is returned.

Related functions are **isalnum()**, **isalpha()**, **isdigit()**, **isgraph()**, **isprint()**, **ispunct()**, and **isspace()**.

isdigit

```
#include <ctype.h>
int isdigit(int ch);
```

The **isdigit()** function returns nonzero if *ch* is a digit, that is, 0 through 9. Otherwise 0 is returned.

Related functions are **isalnum()**, **isalpha()**, **iscntrl()**, **isgraph()**, **isprint()**, **ispunct()**, and **isspace()**.

isgraph

```
#include <ctype.h>
int isgraph(int ch);
```

The **isgraph()** function returns nonzero if *ch* is any printable character other than a space; otherwise 0 is returned. Although implementation dependent, printable characters are generally in the range 0x21 through 0x7E.

Related functions are **isalnum()**, **isalpha()**, **iscntrl()**, **isdigit()**, **isprint()**, **ispunct()**, and **isspace()**.

islower

```
#include <ctype.h>
int islower(int ch);
```

The **islower()** function returns nonzero if *ch* is a lowercase letter; otherwise 0 is returned.

A related function is **isupper()**.

isprint

```
#include <ctype.h>
int isprint(int ch);
```

The **isprint()** function returns nonzero if *ch* is a printable character, including a space; otherwise 0 is returned. Although implementation dependent, printable characters are often in the range 0x20 through 0x7E.

Related functions are **isalnum()**, **isalpha()**, **iscntrl()**, **isdigit()**, **isgraph()**, **ispunct()**, and **isspace()**.

ispunct

```
#include <ctype.h>
int ispunct(int ch);
```

The **ispunct()** function returns nonzero if *ch* is a punctuation character; otherwise 0 is returned. The term "punctuation," as defined by this function, includes all printing characters that are neither alphanumeric nor a space.

Related functions are **isalnum()**, **isalpha()**, **iscntrl()**, **isdigit()**, **isgraph()**, **ispunct()**, and **isspace()**.

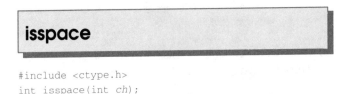

isspace

```
#include <ctype.h>
int isspace(int ch);
```

The **isspace()** function returns nonzero if *ch* is either a space, horizontal tab, vertical tab, formfeed, carriage return, or newline character; otherwise 0 is returned.

Related functions are **isalnum()**, **isalpha()**, **iscntrl()**, **isdigit()**, **isgraph()**, and **ispunct()**.

isupper

```
#include <ctype.h>
int isupper(int ch);
```

The **isupper()** function returns nonzero if *ch* is an uppercase letter; otherwise 0 is returned.

A related function is **islower()**.

isxdigit

```
#include <ctype.h>
int isxdigit(int ch);
```

The **isxdigit()** function returns nonzero if *ch* is a hexadecimal digit; otherwise 0 is returned. A hexadecimal digit will be in one of these ranges: A–F, a–f, or 0–9.

Related functions are **isalnum()**, **isalpha()**, **iscntrl()**, **isdigit()**, **isgraph()**, **ispunct()**, and **isspace()**.

memchr

```
#include "string.h"
void *memchr(const void *buffer, int ch,
             size_t count);
```

The **memchr()** function searches the array pointed to by *buffer* for the first occurrence of *ch* in the first *count* characters.

The **memchr()** function returns a pointer to the first occurrence of *ch* in *buffer*, or it returns a null pointer if *ch* is not found.

Related functions are **memcpy()** and **isspace()**.

memcmp

```
#include <string.h>
int memcmp(const void *buf1, const void
           *buf2, size_t count);
```

The **memcmp()** function compares the first *count* characters of the arrays pointed to by *buf1* and *buf2*. The comparison is done lexicographically.

The **memcmp()** function returns an integer that is interpreted as indicated here:

Value	Meaning
Less than 0	*buf1* is less than *buf2*
0	*buf1* is equal to *buf2*
Greater than 0	*buf1* is greater than *buf2*

Related functions are **memchr()**, **memcpy()**, and **strcmp()**.

memcpy

```
#include <string.h>
void *memcpy(void *to, const void *from,
             size_t count);
```

The **memcpy()** function copies *count* characters from the array pointed to by *from* into the array pointed to by *to*. If the arrays overlap, the behavior of **memcopy()** is undefined.

The **memcpy()** function returns a pointer to *to*.

A related function is **memmove()**.

memmove

```
#include <string.h>
void *memmove(void *to, const void *from,
              size_t count);
```

The **memmove()** function copies *count* characters from the array pointed to by *from* into the array pointed to by *to*. If the arrays overlap, the copy will take place correctly, placing the correct contents into *to* but leaving *from* modified.

The **memmove()** function returns a pointer to *to*.

A related function is **memcpy()**.

memset

```
#include <string.h>
void *memset(void *buf, int ch, size_t count);
```

The **memset()** function copies the low-order byte of *ch* into the first *count* characters of the array pointed to by **buf**. It returns *buf*.

The most common use of **memset()** is to initialize a region of memory to some known value.

Related functions are **memcmp()**, **memcpy()**, and **memmove()**.

strcat

```
#include <string.h>
char *strcat(char *str1, const char *str2);
```

The **strcat()** function concatenates a copy of *str2* to *str1* and terminates *str1* with a null. The null terminator originally ending *str1* is overwritten by the first character of *str2*. The string *str2* is untouched by the operation. If the arrays overlap, the behavior of **strcat()** is undefined.

The **strcat()** function returns *str1*.

Remember, no bounds checking takes place, so it is the programmer's responsibility to ensure that *str1* is large enough to hold both its original contents and also those of *str2*.

Related functions are **strchr()**, **strcmp()**, and **strcpy()**.

strchr

```
#include <string.h>
char *strchr(const char *str, int ch);
```

The **strchr()** function returns a pointer to the first occurrence of the low-order byte of *ch* in the string pointed to by *str*. If no match is found, a null pointer is returned.

Related functions are **strpbrk()**, **strspn()**, **strstr()**, and **strtok()**.

strcmp

```
#include <string.h>
int strcmp(const char *str1, const char *str2);
```

The **strcmp()** function lexicographically compares two strings and returns an integer based on the outcome as shown here:

Value	Meaning
Less than 0	*str1* is less than *str2*
0	*str1* is equal to *str2*
Greater than 0	*str1* is greater than *str2*

Related functions are **strchr()**, **strcpy()**, and **strcmp()**.

strcoll

```
#include <string.h>
int strcoll(const char *str1, const char *str2);
```

The **strcoll()** function compares the string pointed to by *str1* with the one pointed to by *str2*. The comparison is performed in accordance to the locale specified using the **setlocale()** function (see **setlocale** for details).

The **strcoll()** function returns an integer that is interpreted as indicated here:

Value	Meaning
Less than 0	*str1* is less than *str2*
0	*str1* is equal to *str2*
Greater than 0	*str1* is greater than *str2*

Related functions are **memcmp()** and **strcmp()**.

strcpy

```
#include <string.h>
char *strcpy(char *str1, const char *str2);
```

The **strcpy()** function is used to copy the contents of *str2* into *str1*. *str2* must be a pointer to a null-terminated string. The **strcpy()** function returns a pointer to *str1*.

If *str1* and *str2* overlap the behavior of **strcpy()** is undefined.

Related functions are **memcpy()**, **strchr()**, **strcmp()**, and **strncmp()**.

strcspn

```
#include <string.h>
int strcspn(const char *str1, const *str2);
```

The **strcspn()** function returns the length of the initial substring of the string pointed to by *str1* that is made up of only those characters not contained in the string pointed to by *str2*. Stated differently, **strcspn()** returns the index of the first character in the string pointed to by *str1* that matches any of the characters in the string pointed to by *str2*.

Related functions are **strrchr()**, **strpbrk()**, **strstr()**, and **strtok()**.

strerror

```
#include <string.h>
char *strerror(int errnum);
```

The **strerror()** function returns a pointer to an implementation-defined string associated with the value of errnum. Under no circumstances should you modify the string.

strlen

```
#include <string.h>
size_t strlen(char *str);
```

The **strlen()** function returns the length of the null-terminated string pointed to by str. The null is not counted.

Related functions are **memcpy()**, **strchr()**, **strcmp()**, and **strncmp()**.

strncat

```
#include <string.h>
char *strncat(char *str1, const *str2,
             size_t count);
```

The **strncat()** function concatenates not more that count characters of the string pointed to by str2 to the string pointed to by str1 and terminates str1 with a null. The null terminator originally ending str1 is overwritten by the first character of str2. The string str2 is untouched by the operation. If the strings overlap, the behavior is undefined.

The **strncat()** function returns *str1*.

Reminder   No bounds checking takes place, so it is the programmer's responsibility to ensure that *str1* is large enough to hold both its original contents and also those of *str2*.

Related functions are **strcat()**, **strnchr()**, **strncmp()**, and **strncpy()**.

strncmp

```
#include <string.h>
int strncmp(const char *str1, const char
            *str2, size_t count);
```

The **strncmp()** function lexicographically compares not more that *count* characters from the two null-terminated strings and returns an integer based on the outcome, as shown here:

Value	Meaning
Less than 0	*str1* is less than *str2*
0	*str1* is equal to *str2*
Greater than 0	*str1* is greater than *str2*

If there are less than *count* characters in either string, the comparison ends when the first null is encountered.

Related functions are **strcmp()**, **strnchr()**, and **strncpy()**.

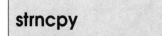

strncpy

```
#include <string.h>
char *strncpy(char *str1, const char *str2,
              size_t count);
```

The **strncpy()** function is used to copy up to *count* characters from the string pointed to by *str2* into the string pointed to by *str1*. *str2* must be a pointer to a null-terminated string.

If *str1* and *str2* overlap, the behavior of **strncpy()** is undefined.

If the string pointed to by *str2* has less than *count* characters, nulls will be appended to the end of *str1* until *count* characters have been copied.

Alternatively, if the string pointed to by *str2* is longer than *count* characters, the resultant string pointed to by *str1* will not be null terminated.

The **strncpy()** function returns a pointer to *str1*.

Related functions are **memcpy()**, **strchr()**, **strncat()**, and **strncmp()**.

strpbrk

```
#include <string.h>
char *strpbrk(const char *str1, const char *str2);
```

The **strpbrk()** function returns a pointer to the first character in the string pointed to by *str1* that matches any character in the string pointed to by *str2*. The null terminators are not included. If there are no matches, a null pointer is returned.

Related functions are **strspn()**, **strrchr()**, **strstr()**, and **strtok()**.

strrchr

```
#include <string.h>
char *strrchr(const char *str, int ch);
```

The **strrchr()** function returns a pointer to the last occurrence of the low-order byte of *ch* in the string pointed to by *str*. If no match is found, a null pointer is returned.

Related functions are **strpbrk()**, **strspn()**, **strstr()**, and **strtok()**.

strspn

```
#include <string.h>
size_t strspn(const char *str1, const char *str2);
```

The **strspn()** function returns the length of the initial substring of the string pointed to by *str1* that is made up of only those characters contained in the string pointed to by *str2*. Stated differently, **strspn()** returns the index of the first character in the string pointed to by *str1* that does not match any of the characters in the string pointed to by *str2*.

Related functions are **strpbrk()**, **strrchr()**, **strstr()**, and **strtok()**.

strstr

```
#include <string.h>
char *strstr(const char *str1, const char *str2);
```

The **strstr()** function returns a pointer to the first occurrence in the string pointed to by *str1* of the string pointed to by *str2*. It returns a null pointer if no match is found.

Related functions are **strchr()**, **strcspn()**, **strpbrk()**, **strspn()**, **strtok()**, and **strrchr()**.

strtok

```
#inlude <string.h>
char *strtok(char *str1, const char *str2);
```

The **strtok()** function returns a pointer to the next token in the string pointed to by *str1*. The characters making up the string pointed to by *str2* are the delimiters that may terminate the token. A null pointer is returned when there is no token to return.

The first time **strtok()** is called, *str1* is actually used in the call. Subsequent calls must use a null pointer for the first argument.

It is important to understand that the **strtok()** function modifies the string pointed to by *str1*. Each time a token is found, a null is placed where the delimiter was found. In this way **strtok()** can continue to advance through the string.

It is possible to use a different set of delimiters for each call to **strtok()**.

Related functions are **strchr()**, **strcspn()**, **strpbrk()**, **strrchr()**, and **strspn()**.

strxfrm

```
#include <string.h>
size_t strxfrm(char *str1, const char *str2,
               size_t count);
```

The **strxfrm()** function transforms the first *count* characters of the string pointed to by *str2* so that it can be used by the **strcmp()** function and puts the result into the string pointed to by *str1*. After the transformation, the outcome of a **strcmp()** using *str1* and a **strcoll()** using the original string pointed to by *str2* will be the same. The main use for this function is in foreign language environments that do not use the ASCII collating sequence.

The **strxfrm()** function returns the length of the transformed string.

A related function is **strcoll()**.

tolower

```
#include <ctype.h>
int tolower(int ch);
```

The **tolower()** function returns the lowercase equivalent
of *ch* if *ch* is a letter; otherwise *ch* is returned
unchanged.

A related function is **toupper()**.

toupper

```
#include <ctype.h>
int toupper(int ch);
```

The **toupper()** function returns the uppercase equivalent
of *ch* if *ch* is a letter; otherwise *ch* is return unchanged.

A related function is **tolower()**.

Mathematical Functions

The C++ standard library contains several mathematical functions, which fall into the following categories:

- Trigonometric functions
- Hyperbolic functions
- Exponential and logarithmic functions
- Miscellaneous functions

All the math functions require the header file MATH.H to be included in any program using them. In addition to declaring the math functions, this header defines three macros called **EDOM**, **ERANGE**, and **HUGE_VAL**. If an argument to a math function is not in the domain for which it is defined, an implementation-defined value is returned, and the built-in global integer variable **errno** is set equal to **EDOM**. If a routine produces a result that is too large to be represented by a **double**, an overflow occurs. This causes the routine to return **HUGE_VAL**, and **errno** is set to **ERANGE**, indicating a range error. If an underflow happens, the routine returns 0 and sets **errno** to **ERANGE**.

acos

```
#include <math.h>
double acos(double arg);
```

The **acos()** function returns the arccosine of *arg*. The argument to **acos()** must be in the range –1 to 1; otherwise a domain error will occur.

Related functions are **asin()**, **atan()**, **atan2()**, **sin()**, **cos()**, **tan()**, **sinh()**, **cosh()**, and **tanh()**.

asin

```
#include <math.h>
double asin(double arg);
```

The **asin()** function returns the arcsine of *arg*. The argument to **asin()** must be in the range −1 to 1; otherwise a domain error will occur.

Related functions are **acos()**, **atan()**, **atan2()**, **sin()**, **cos()**, **tan()**, **sinh()**, **cosh()**, and **tanh()**.

atan

```
#include <math.h>
double atan(double arg);
```

The **atan()** function returns the arctangent of *arg*.

Related functions are **asin()**, **acos()**, **atan2()**, **tan()**, **cos()**, **sin()**, **sinh()**, **cosh()**, and **tanh()**.

atan2

```
#include <math.h>
double atan2(double y, double x);
```

The **atan2()** function returns the arctangent of *y/x*. It uses the signs of its arguments to compute the quadrant of the return value.

Related functions are **asin()**, **acos()**, **atan()**, **tan()**, **cos()**, **sin()**, **sinh()**, **cosh()**, and **tanh()**.

ceil

```
#include <math.h>
double ceil(double num);
```

The **ceil()** function returns the smallest integer (represented as a **double**) not less than *num*. For example, given 1.02, **ceil()** would return 2.0. Given −1.02, **ceil()** would return −1.

Related functions are **floor()** and **fmod()**.

cos

```
#include <math.h>
double cos(double arg);
```

The **cos()** function returns the cosine of *arg*. The value of *arg* must be in radians.

Related functions are **asin()**, **acos()**, **atan2()**, **atan()**, **tan()**, **sin()**, **sinh()**, **cos()**, and **tanh()**.

cosh

```
#include <math.h>
double cosh(double arg);
```

The **cosh()** function returns the hyperbolic cosine of *arg*. The value of *arg* must be in radians.

Related functions are **asin()**, **acos()**, **atan2()**, **atan()**, **tan()**, **sin()**, **cosh()**, and **tanh()**.

exp

```
#include <math.h>
double exp(double arg);
```

The **exp()** function returns the natural logarithm *e* raised to the *arg* power.

A related function is **log()**.

fabs

```
#include <math.h>
double fabs(double num);
```

The **fabs()** function returns the absolute value of *num*.

A related function is **abs()**.

floor

```
#include <math.h>
double floor(double num);
```

The **floor()** function returns the largest integer (represented as a **double**) not greater than num. For example, given 1.02, **floor()** would return 1.0. Given −1.02, **floor()** would return −2.0.

Related functions are **fceil()** and **fmod()**.

fmod

```
#include <math.h>
double fmod(double x, double y);
```

The **fmod()** function returns the remainder of x/y.

Related functions are **ceil()**, **floor()**, and **fabs()**.

frexp

```
#include <math.h>
double frexp(double num, int *exp);
```

The **frexp()** function decomposes the number num into a mantissa in the range 0.5 to less than 1, and an integer exponent such that $num = mantissa * 2^{exp}$. The mantissa is returned by the function, and the exponent is stored at the variable pointed to by exp.

A related function is **ldexp()**.

ldexp

```
#include <math.h>
double ldexp(double num, int exp);
```

The **ldexp()** returns the value of *num* * 2^*exp*. If overflow occurs, **HUGE_VAL** is returned.

Related functions are **frexp()** and **modf()**.

log

```
#include <math.h>
double log(double num);
```

The **log()** function returns the natural logarithm for *num*. A domain error occurs if *num* is negative, and a range error occurs if the argument is 0.

A related function is **log10()**.

log10

```
#include <math.h>
double log10(double num);
```

The **log10()** function returns the base 10 logarithm for *num*. A domain error occurs if *num* is negative, and a range error occurs if the argument is 0.

A related function is **log()**.

modf

```
#include <math.h>
double modf(double num, int *i);
```

The **modf()** function decomposes *num* into its integer and fractional parts. It returns the fractional portion and places the integer part in the variable pointed to by *i*.

Related functions are **frexp()** and **ldexp()**.

pow

```
#include <math.h>
double pow(double base, double exp);
```

The **pow()** function returns *base* raised to the *exp* power *(base^{exp})*. A domain error occurs if *base* is 0 and *exp* is less than or equal to 0. It will also happen if *base* is negative and *exp* is not an integer. An overflow produces a range error.

Related functions are **exp()**, **log()**, and **sqrt()**.

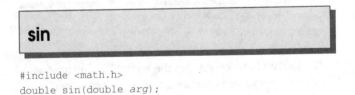

sin

```
#include <math.h>
double sin(double arg);
```

The **sin()** function returns the sine of *arg*. The value of *arg* must be in radians.

Related functions are **asin()**, **acos()**, **atan2()**, **atan()**, **tan()**, **cos()**, **sinh()**, **cosh()**, and **tanh()**.

sinh

```
#include <math.h>
double sinh(double arg);
```

The **sinh()** function returns the hyperbolic sine of *arg*. The value of *arg* must be in radians.

Related functions are **asin()**, **acos()**, **atan2()**, **atan()**, **tan()**, **cos()**, **tanh()**, **cosh()**, and **sin()**.

sqrt

```
#include <math.h>
double sqrt(double num);
```

The **sqrt()** function returns the square root of *num*. If it is called with a negative argument, a domain error will occur.

Related functions are **exp()**, **log()**, and **pow()**.

tan

```
#include <math.h>
double tan(double arg);
```

The **tan()** function returns the tangent of *arg*. The value of *arg* must be in radians.

Related functions are **acos()**, **asin()**, **atan()**, **atan2()**, **cos()**, **sin()**, **sinh()**, **cosh()**, and **tanh()**.

tanh

```
#include <math.h>
double tanh(double arg);
```

The **tanh()** function returns the hyperbolic tangent of *arg*. The value of *arg* must be in radians.

Related functions are **acos()**, **asin()**, **atan()**, **atan2()**, **cos()**, **sin()**, **cosh()**, **sinh()**, and **tan()**.

Time, Date, and Other System-Related Functions

This section covers those functions that in one way or another are more sensitive to the operating system than others. These include the time and date functions and those functions that relate to the geographical location in which the computer is used.

Standard C++ defines several functions that deal with the date and time of the system as well as elapsed time. These functions require the header file TIME.H. This header defines three types: **clock_t**, **time_t**, and **tm**. The types **clock_t** and **time_t** are capable of representing the system time and date as a long integer. This is called the *calendar time*. The structure type **tm** holds the date and time broken down into its elements. The **tm** structure is defined as shown here:

```
struct tm {
  int tm_sec;   /* seconds, 0-59 */
  int tm_min;   /* minutes, 0-59 */
  int tm_hour;  /* hours, 0-23 */
  int tm_mday;  /* day of the month, 1-31 */
  int tm_mon;   /* months since Jan, 0-11 */
  int tm_year;  /* years from 1900 */
  int tm_wday;  /* days since Sunday, 0-6 */
  int tm_yday;  /* days since Jan 1, 0-365 */
  int tm_isdst  /* Daylight Savings Time
                   indicator */
}
```

The value of **tm_isdst** will be positive if Daylight Savings Time is in effect, 0 if it is not in effect, and negative if there is no information available. This form of the time and date is called the *broken-down time*.

In addition, TIME.H defines the macro **CLK_TCK**, which is the number of system clock ticks per second.

The geographical location functions require the header file LOCALE.H.

Most C++ compilers will also supply operating system and computer-specific functions, so be sure to check the user's manual for your compiler for these types of functions.

asctime

```
#include <time.h>
char *asctime(struct tm *ptr);
```

The **asctime()** function returns a pointer to a string that converts the information stored in the structure pointed to by *ptr* into the following form.

day month date hours:minutes:seconds year\n\0

For example:

```
Wed Jun 19 12:05:34 1999
```

The structure pointer passed to **asctime()** is generally obtained from either **localtime()** or **gmtime()**.

The buffer used by **asctime()** to hold the formatted output string is a statically allocated character array and is overwritten each time the function is called. If you wish to save the contents of the string, you must copy it elsewhere.

Related functions are **localtime()**, **gmtime()**, **time()**, and **ctime()**.

clock

```
#include <time.h>
clock_t clock(void);
```

The **clock()** function returns a value that approximates the amount of time the calling program has been running. To transform this value into seconds, divide it by **CLK_TCK**. A value of −1 is returned if the time is not available.

Related functions are **time()**, **asctime()**, and **ctime()**.

ctime

```
#include <time.h>
char *ctime(const time_t *time);
```

The **ctime()** function returns a pointer to a string of the form

day month year hours:minutes:seconds year\n\0

given a pointer to the calendar time. The calendar time is generally obtained through a call to **time()**.

The buffer used by **ctime()** to hold the formatted output string is a statically allocated character array and is overwritten each time the function is called. If you wish to save the contents of the string, it is necessary to copy it elsewhere.

Related functions are **localtime()**, **gmtime()**, **time()**, and **asctime()**.

difftime

```
#include <time.h>
double difftime(time_t time2, time_t time1);
```

The **difftime()** function returns the difference, in seconds, between *time1* and *time2*. That is, *time2 − time1*.

Related functions are **localtime()**, **gmtime()**, **time()**, **asctime()**.

gmtime

```
#include <time.h>
struct tm *gmtime(time_t *time);
```

The **gmtime()** function returns a pointer to the broken-down form of *time* in the form of a **tm** structure. The time is represented in Greenwich mean time. The *time* value is generally obtained through a call to **time()**.

The structure used by **gmtime()** to hold the broken-down time is statically allocated and is overwritten each time the function is called. If you wish to save the contents of the structure, you must copy it elsewhere.

Related functions are **localtime()**, **time()**, and **asctime()**.

localeconv

```
#include <locale.h>
struct lconv *localeconv(void);
```

The **localeconv()** function returns a pointer to a structure of type **lconv**, which contains various country-specific environmental information relating to the way numbers are formatted. The **lconv** structure is organized as shown here:

```
struct lconv {
  char *decimal_point; /* decimal point character
                          for nonmonetary values */
  char *thousands_sep; /* thousands separator
                          for nonmonetary
                          values */
  char *grouping; /* specifies grouping for
                     nonmonetary values */
  char int_curr_symbol; /* international
                           currency symbol */
  char *currency_symbol; /* local currency
                            symbol */
  char *mon_decimal_point; /* decimal point
                              character for
                              monetary
                              values */
  char *mon_thousands_sep; /* thousands
                              separator
                              for monetary
                              values */
  char *mon_grouping; /* specifies grouping
                         for monetary values */
  char *positive_sign; /* positive value
                          indicator for
                          monetary values */
```

```
    char *negative_sign; /* negative value
                            indicator for
                            monetary values */
    char int_frac_digits; /* number of digits
                             displayed to the
                             right of the
                             decimal point for
                             monetary values
                             displayed using
                             international
                             format */
    char frac_digits; /* number of digits
                         displayed to the
                         right of the decimal
                         point for monetary
                         values displayed using
                         local format */
    char p_cs_precedes; /* 1 if currency symbol
                           precedes positive
                           value, 0 if
                           currency symbol
                           follows value */
    char p_sep_by_space; /* 1 if currency symbol
                            is separated
                            from value by a space,
                            0 otherwise */
    char n_cs_precedes; /* 1 if currency symbol
                           precedes a negative
                           value, 0 if currency
                           symbol follows value */
    char n_sep_by_space; /* 1 if currency symbol
                            is separated from
                            a negative value
                            by a space, 0 if
                            currency symbol
                            follows value */
    char p_sign_posn; /* indicates position of
                         positive value symbol */
    char n_sign_posn; /* indicates position of
                         negative value symbol */
}
```

The **localeconv()** function returns a pointer to the **conv** structure. You must not alter the contents of this structure. Refer to your compiler manual for implementation-specific information relating to this function.

A related function is **setlocale()**.

localtime

```
#include <time.h>
struct tm *localtime(const time_t *time);
```

The **localtime()** function returns a pointer to the broken-down form of *time* in the form of a **tm** structure. The time is represented in local time. The *time* value is generally obtained through a call to **time()**.

The structure used by **localtime()** to hold the broken-down time is statically allocated and is overwritten each time the function is called. If you wish to save the contents of the structure, you must copy it elsewhere.

Related functions are **gmtime()**, **time()**, and **asctime()**.

mktime

```
#include <time.h>
time_t mktime(struct tm *time);
```

The **mktime()** function returns the calendar-time equivalent of the broken-down time found in the structure pointed to by *time*. This function is primarily used to initialize the system time. The elements **tm_wday** and **tm_yday** are set by the function, so they need not be defined at the time of the call.

If **mktime()** cannot represent the information as a valid calendar time, −1 is returned.

Related functions are **time()**, **gmtime()**, **asctime()**, and **ctime()**.

setlocale

```
#include <locale.h>
char *setlocale(int type, const char *locale);
```

The **setlocale()** function allows certain parameters that are sensitive to the geographical location of a program's execution to be queried or set. For example, in Europe, the comma is used in place of the decimal point.

If *locale* is null, **setlocale()** returns a pointer to the current localization string. Otherwise, **setlocale()** attempts to use the specified localization string to set the locale parameters as specified by *type*.

At the time of the call, *type* must be one of the following macros:

LC_ALL
LC_COLLATE
LC_CTYPE
LC_MONETARY
LC_NUMERIC
LC_TIME

LC_ALL refers to all localization categories.
LC_COLLATE affects the operation of the **strcoll()**

function. **LC_CTYPE** alters the way the character functions work. **LC_MONETARY** determines the monetary format. **LC_NUMERIC** changes the decimal-point character for formatted input/output functions. Finally, **LC_TIME** determines the behavior of the **strftime()** function.

The ANSI C standard defines two possible strings for *locale*. The first is "C", which specifies a minimal environment for C compilation. The second is " ", the null string, which specifies the implementation-defined default environment. All other values for *locale* are implementation defined and will affect portability.

The **setlocale()** function returns a pointer to a string associated with the *type* parameter.

Related functions are **localeconv()**, **time()**, **strcoll()**, and **strftime()**.

strftime

```
#include <time.h>
size_t strftime(char *str, size_t maxsize,
                char const *fmt,
                const struct tm *time);
```

The **strftime()** function places time and date information, along with other information, into the string pointed to by *str* according to the format commands found in the string pointed to by *fmt* and using the broken-down time *time*. A maximum of *maxsize* characters will be placed into *str*.

The **strftime()** function works a little like **sprintf()** in that it recognizes a set of format commands that begin with the percent sign (%) and it places its formatted output into a string. The format commands are used to specify the exact way various time and date information is represented in *str*. Any other characters found in the format string are placed into *str* unchanged. The time and date displayed are in local time. The format commands are shown in the table below. Notice that many of the commands are case sensitive.

The **strftime()** function returns the number of characters placed in the string pointed to by *str* or 0 if an error occurs.

Command	Replaced By
%a	Abbreviated weekday name
%A	Full weekday name
%b	Abbreviated month name
%B	Full month name
%c	Standard date and time string
%d	Day of month as a decimal (1–31)
%H	Hour (0–23)
%I	Hour (1–12)
%j	Day of year as a decimal (1–366)
%m	Month as decimal (1–12)
%M	Minute as decimal (0–59)
%p	Locale's equivalent of AM or PM
%S	Second as decimal (0–59)
%U	Week of year, Sunday being first day (0–52)
%w	Weekday as a decimal (0–6, Sunday being 0)
%W	Week of year, Monday being first day (0–52)

Command	Replaced By
%x	Standard date string
%X	Standard time string
%y	Year in decimal without century (00–99)
%Y	Year including century as decimal
%Z	Time zone name
%%	The percent sign

Related functions are **time()**, **localtime()**, and **gmtime()**.

time

```
#include <time.h>
time_t time(time_t *time);
```

The **time()** function returns the current calendar time of the system. If the system has no time, –1 is returned.

The **time()** function can be called either with a null pointer or with a pointer to a variable of type **time_t**. If the latter is used, the variable will also be assigned the calendar time.

Related functions are **localtime()**, **gmtime()**, **strftime()**, and **ctime()**.

Dynamic Allocation

There are two ways in which a C++ program can dynamically allocate memory. The first uses C++'s standard dynamic allocation functions. These functions were first defined by the C language and are not object oriented. The second way that you may dynamically allocate memory is to use C++'s **new** and **delete** operators. There are several advantages to using C++'s dynamic allocation operators. First, **new** automatically allocates the correct amount of memory for the type of data being allocated. Second, it returns the correct type of pointer to that memory. Third, both **new** and **delete** can be overloaded.

Since **new** and **delete** have advantages over using C++'s dynamic allocation functions, their use is recommended. However, since much existing code uses the traditional allocation functions, they are discussed here.

Note For a discussion of **new** and **delete**, see "Keyword Summary."

At the core of C++'s traditional dynamic allocation system are the functions **malloc()** and **free()**, which are part of the standard library. Each time a **malloc()** memory request is made, a portion of the remaining free memory is allocated. Each time a **free()** memory release call is made, memory is returned to the system. The most common way to implement **malloc()** and **free()** is to organize the free memory into a linked list. However, the memory management method is implementation dependent. The prototypes for the dyanmic allocation functions are in STDLIB.H. The dynamic allocation system returns **void** pointers. This means that you must use a type cast when assigning them to another type of pointer.

All C++ compilers will include at least these four
dynamic allocation functions: **calloc()**, **malloc()**, **free()**,
realloc(). However, if your computer uses a processor
from the 8086 family, your compiler will almost certainly
contain several variants on these functions to
accommodate the segmented memory used by these
processors. If this is the case, refer to your compiler's
user manual.

calloc

```
#include <stdlib.h>
void *calloc(size_t num, size_t size);
```

The **calloc()** function allocates memory the size of which
is equal to *num * size*. That is, **calloc()** allocates
sufficient memory for an array of *num* objects of size *size*.

The **calloc()** function returns a pointer to the first byte of
the allocated region. If there is not enough memory to
satisfy the request, a null pointer is returned. It is
always important to verify that the return value is not a
null pointer before attempting to use it.

Related functions are **free()**, **malloc()**, and **realloc()**.

free

```
#include <stdlib.h>
void free(void *ptr);
```

The **free()** function returns the memory pointed to by *ptr*
to the heap. This makes the memory available for future
allocation.

It is imperative that **free()** only be called with a pointer that was previously allocated using one of the dynamic allocation system's functions (either **malloc()** or **calloc()**). Using an invalid pointer in the call most likely will destroy the memory management mechanism and cause a system crash.

Related functions are **calloc()**, **malloc()**, and **realloc()**.

malloc

```
#include <stdlib.h>
void *malloc(size_t size);
```

The **malloc()** function returns a pointer to the first byte of a region of memory of size *size* that has been allocated from the heap. If there is insufficient memory in the heap to satisfy the request, **malloc()** returns a null pointer. It is always important to verify that the return value is not a null pointer before attempting to use it. Attempting to use a null pointer will usually result in a system crash.

Related functions are **free()**, **realloc()**, and **calloc()**.

realloc

```
#include <stdlib.h>
void *realloc(void *ptr, size_t size);
```

The **realloc()** function changes the size of the previously allocated memory pointed to by *ptr* to that specified by *size*. The value of *size* may be greater or less than the original. A pointer to the memory block is returned because it may be necessary for **realloc()** to move the block in order to increase its size. If this occurs, the contents of the old block are copied into the new block—no information is lost.

If *ptr* is null, **realloc()** simply allocates *size* bytes of memory and returns a pointer to it. If *size* is 0, the memory pointed to by *ptr* is freed.

If there is not enough free memory in the heap to allocate *size* bytes, a null pointer is returned, and the original block is left unchanged.

Related functions are **free()**, **malloc()**, and **calloc()**.

Miscellaneous Functions

The functions discussed in this chapter don't easily fit into any other category. They include various conversion, variable-length argument processing, sorting, and other functions.

Many of the functions covered here require the use of the header STDLIB.H. In this header are defined the two types, **div_t** and **ldiv_t**, which are the types of the values returned by **div()** and **ldiv()**, respectively. Also defined is the type **size_t**, which is the unsigned value returned by **sizeof**. These macros are also defined, as follows:

Macro	Meaning
NULL	A null pointer
RAND_MAX	The maximum value that can be returned by the **rand()** function
EXIT_FAILURE	The value returned to calling process if program termination is unsuccessful
EXIT_SUCCESS	The value returned to calling process if program termination is successful

If a function requires a different header file than STDLIB.H, that function description will discuss it.

abort

```
#include <stdlib.h>
void abort(void);
```

The **abort()** function causes immediate abnormal termination of a program. Generally, no files are flushed. In environments that support it, **abort()** will return an implementation-defined value to the calling process (usually the operating system) indicating failure.

Related functions are **exit()** and **atexit()**.

abs

```
#include <stdlib.h>
int abs(int num);
```

The **abs()** function returns the absolute value of the integer num.

A related function is **labs()**.

assert

```
#include <assert.h>
void assert(int exp);
```

The **assert()** macro, defined in its header ASSERT.H, writes error information to **stderr** and then aborts program execution if the expression exp evaluates to 0. Otherwise, **assert()** does nothing. Although the exact output is implementation defined, many compilers use a message similar to this:

Assertion failed: <*expression*>, file <*file*>, line <*linenum*>

The **assert()** macro is generally used to help verify that a program is operating correctly, with the expression being devised in such a way that it evaluates to true only when no errors have taken place.

It is not necessary to remove the **assert()** statements from the source code once a program is debugged because if the macro **NDEBUG** is defined (as anything), the **assert()** macros will be ignored.

A related function is **abort()**.

atexit

```
#include <stdlib.h>
int atexit(void (*func)(void));
```

The **atexit()** function causes the function pointed to by *func* to be called upon normal program termination. That is, at the end of a program run, the specified function will be called.

The **atexit()** function returns 0 if the function is successfully registered as a termination function, nonzero otherwise.

At least 32 termination functions may be established, and they will be called in the reverse order of their establishment.

Related functions are **exit()** and **abort()**.

atof

```
#include <stdlib.h>
double atof(const char *str);
```

The **atof()** function converts the string pointed to by *str* into a **double** value. The string must contain a valid floating point number. If this is not the case, the returned value is undefined.

The number may be terminated by any character that cannot be part of a valid floating point number. This includes white space, punctuation (other than periods), and characters other than E or e. This means that if **atof()** is called with "100.00HELLO", the value 100.00 will be returned.

Related functions are **atoi()** and **atol()**.

atoi

```
#include <stdlib.h>
int atoi(const char *str);
```

The **atoi()** function converts the string pointed to by *str* into an **int** value. The string must contain a valid integer number. If this is not the case, the returned value is undefined; however, most implementations will return 0.

The number may be terminated by any character that cannot be part of an integer number. This includes white space, punctuation, and characters other than E or e. This means that if **atoi()** is called with "123.23", the integer value 123 will be returned, and the 0.23 is ignored.

Related functions are **atof()** and **atol()**.

atol

```
#include <stdlib.h>
long atol(const char *str);
```

The **atol()** function converts the string pointed to by *str* into a **long** value. The string must contain a valid long integer number. If this is not the case, the returned value is undefined; however, most implementations will return 0.

The number may be terminated by any character that cannot be part of an integer number. This includes white space, punctuation, and characters other than E or e. This means that if **atol()** is called with "123.23", the integer value 123 will be returned, and the 0.23 is ignored.

Related functions are **atof()** and **atoi()**.

bsearch

```
#include <stdlib.h>
void *bsearch(const void *key, const void
              *buf, size_t num, size_t size,
              int (*compare)(const void *,
              const void *));
```

The **bsearch()** function performs a binary search on the sorted array pointed to by *buf* and returns a pointer to the first member that matches the key pointed to by *key*. The number of elements in the array is specified by *num*, and the size (in bytes) of each element is described by *size*.

The function pointed to by *compare* is used to compare an element of the array with the key. The form of the *compare* function must be as follows:

int *func_name*(const void **arg1*, const void **arg2*);

It must return values as described in the following table:

Comparison	Value Returned
arg1 is less than *arg2*	Less than 0
arg1 is equal to *arg2*	0
arg1 is greater than *arg2*	Greater than 0

The array must be sorted in ascending order with the lowest address containing the lowest element.

If the array does not contain the key, a null pointer is returned.

A related function is **qsort()**.

div

```
#include <stdlib.h>
div_t div(int numerator, int denominator);
```

The **div()** function returns the quotient and the remainder of the operation *numerator / denominator* in a structure of type **div_t**.

The structure type **div_t** is defined in STDLIB.H and will have at least these two fields:

```
int quot;  /* the quotient */
int rem;   /* the remainder */
```

A related function is **ldiv()**.

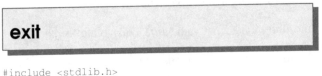

exit

```
#include <stdlib.h>
void exit(int exit_code);
```

The **exit()** function causes immediate, normal termination of a program.

The value of *exit_code* is passed to the calling process, usually the operating system, if the environment supports it. By convention, if the value of *exit_code* is 0—or **EXIT_SUCCESS**—normal program termination is assumed. A nonzero value or **EXIT_FAILURE** is used to indicate an implementation-defined error.

Related functions are **atexit()** and **abort()**.

getenv

```
#include <stdlib.h>
char *getenv(const char *name);
```

The **getenv()** function returns a pointer to environmental information associated with the string pointed to by *name* in the implementation-defined environmental information table. The string returned must never be changed by the program.

The environment of a program may include such things as path names and devices online. The exact nature of this data is implementation defined. You will need to refer to your compiler's user manual for details.

If a call is made to **getenv()** with an argument that does not match any of the environment data, a null pointer is returned.

A related function is **system()**.

labs

```
#include <stdlib.h>
long labs(long num);
```

The **labs()** function returns the absolute value of the variable *num*.

A related function is **abs()**.

ldiv

```
#include <stdlib.h>
ldiv_t ldiv(long numerator, long denominator);
```

The **ldiv()** function returns the quotient and the remainder of the operation *numerator / denominator*.

The structure type **ldiv_t** is defined in STDLIB.H and will have at least these two fields:

```
long quot;   /* the quotient */
long rem;    /* the remainder */
```

A related function is **div()**.

longjmp

```
#include <setjmp.h>
void longjmp(jmp_buf envbuf, int status);
```

The **longjmp()** function causes program execution to resume at the point of the last call to **setjmp()**. These two functions are C++'s way of providing for a jump between functions. Notice that the header SETJUMP.H is required.

The **longjmp()** function operates by resetting the stack to the state as described in *envbuf*, which must have been set by a prior call to **setjmp()**. This causes program execution to resume at the statement following the **setjmp()** invocation. That is, the computer is "tricked" into thinking that it never left the function that called **setjmp()**. (As a somewhat graphic explanation, the **longjmp()** function sort of "warps" across time and (memory) space to a previous point in your program without having to perform the normal function return process.)

The buffer *evnbuf* is of type **jmp_buf**, which is defined in the header SETJMP.H. The buffer must have been set through a call to **setjmp()** prior to calling **longjmp()**.

The value of *status* becomes the return value of **setjump()** and may be interrogated to determine where the long jump came from. The only value that is not allowed is 0.

Note   It is important to understand that the **longjmp()** function must be called before the function that called **setjmp()** returns. If not, the result is technically undefined. (Actually, a crash will almost certainly occur.)

By far the most common use of **longjmp()** is to return from a deeply nested set of routines when an error occurs.

A related function is **setjmp()**.

qsort

```
#include <stdlib.h>
void qsort(void *buf, size_t num, size_t
           size, int (*compare)
           (const void *, const void *));
```

The **qsort()** function sorts the array pointed to by *buf* using a Quicksort (developed by C.A.R. Hoare). The Quicksort is generally considered the best general-purpose sorting algorithm. Upon termination, the array will be sorted. The number of elements in the array is specified by *num*, and the size (in bytes) of each element is described by *size*.

The function pointed to by *compare* is used to compare an element of the array with the key. The form of the *compare* function must be as follows:

int *func_name*(const void *arg1*, const void *arg2*);

It must return values as described here:

Comparison	Value Returned
arg1 is less than *arg2*	Less than 0
arg1 is equal to *arg2*	0
arg1 is greater than *arg2*	Greater than 0

The array is sorted into ascending order with the lowest address containing the lowest element.

A related function is **bsearch()**.

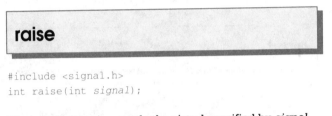

raise

```
#include <signal.h>
int raise(int signal);
```

The **raise()** function sends the signal specified by *signal* to the executing program. It returns 0 if successful; nonzero otherwise. Its uses the header file SIGNAL.H.

A related function is **signal()**.

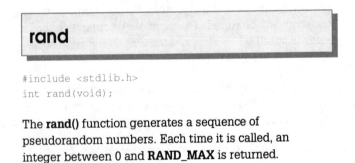

rand

```
#include <stdlib.h>
int rand(void);
```

The **rand()** function generates a sequence of pseudorandom numbers. Each time it is called, an integer between 0 and **RAND_MAX** is returned.

A related function is **srand()**.

setjmp

```
#include <setjmp.h>
int setjmp(jmp_buf envbuf);
```

The **setjmp()** function saves the contents of the system stack in the buffer *envbuf* for later use by **longjmp()**. It uses the header file SETJMP.H.

The **setjmp()** function returns 0 upon invocation. However, a **longjmp()** passes an argument to **setjmp()** when it executes, and it is this value (always nonzero) that will appear to be the value of **setjmp()** after a call to **longjmp()**.

See **longjmp** for additional information.

A related function is **longjmp()**.

signal

```
#include <signal.h>
void (*signal(int signal, void (*func)(int)))
      (int);
```

The **signal()** function defines the function, *func*, to be executed if the specified signal *signal* is received. The operation of this function is somewhat implementation specific.

The value of *func* may be the address of a function or one of the following macros, defined in SIGNAL.H:

Macro	Meaning
SIG_DFL	Use default signal handling
SIG_IGN	Ignore the signal

If a function address is used, the specified function will be executed.

A related function is **raise()**.

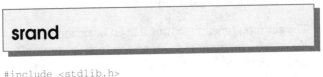

srand

```
#include <stdlib.h>
void srand(unsigned seed);
```

The **srand()** function is used to set a starting point for the sequence generated by **rand()**. (The **rand()** function returns pseudorandom numbers.)

srand() is generally used to allow multiple program runs using different sequences of pseudorandom numbers by specifying different starting points. However, you can generate the same pseudorandom sequence over and over again by calling **srand()** with the same seed before starting the sequence each time.

A related function is **rand()**.

strtod

```
#include <stdlib.h>
double strtod(const char *start, char **end);
```

The **strtod()** function converts the string representation of a number stored in the string pointed to by *start* into a **double** and returns the result.

The **strtod()** function works as follows. First, any white space in the string pointed to by *start* is stripped. Next, each character that comprises the number is read. Any character that cannot be part of a floating point number will cause this process to stop. This includes white space, punctuation (other than periods), and characters other than E or e. Finally, *end* is set to point to the remainder, if any, of the original string. This means that if **strtod()** is called with " 100.00 Pliers", the value 100.00 will be returned and *end* will point to the space that precedes "Pliers".

If a conversion error occurs, **strtod()** returns either **HUGE_VAL** for overflow, or –**HUGE_VAL** for underflow. If no conversion could take place, 0 is returned. In either case, the global variable **errno** is set to **ERANGE**, indicating a range error.

A related function is **atof()**.

strtol

```
#include <stdlib.h>
long strtol(const char *start, char **end,
            int radix);
```

The **strtol()** function converts the string representation of a number stored in the string pointed to by *start* into a **long** and returns the result. The base of the number is determined by *radix*. If *radix* is 0, the base is determined by rules that govern constant specification. If the radix is other than 0, it must be in the range 2 through 36.

The **strtol()** function works as follows. First, any white space in the string pointed to by *start* is stripped. Next, each character that comprises the number is read. Any character that cannot be part of a long integer number will cause this process to stop. This includes white space, punctuation, and characters. Finally, *end* is set to point to the remainder, if any, of the original string. This means that if **strtol()** is called with " 100 Pliers", the value 100L will be returned, and *end* will point to the space that precedes "Pliers".

If a conversion error occurs, **strtol()** returns either **LONG_MAX** for overflow or **LONG_MIN** for underflow, and the global **errno** is set to **ERANGE**, indicating a range error. If no conversion could take place, 0 is returned.

A related function is **atol()**.

strtoul

```
#include <stdlib.h>
unsigned long strtoul(char *start, char
                      **end, int radix);
```

The **strtoul()** function converts the string representation of a number stored in the string pointed to by *start* into an **unsigned long** and returns the result. The base of the number is determined by *radix*. If *radix* is 0, the base is determined by rules that govern constant specification. If the radix is specified, it must be in the range 2 through 36.

The **strtoul()** function works as follows. First, any white space in the string pointed to by *start* is stripped. Next, each character that comprises the number is read. Any character that cannot be part of an unsigned long integer number will cause this process to stop. This includes white space, punctuation, and characters. Finally, *end* is set to point to the remainder, if any, of the original string. This means that if **strtoul()** is called with " 100 Pliers", the value 100L will be returned, and *end* will point to the space that precedes "Pliers".

If a conversion error occurs, **strtoul()** returns either
ULONG_MAX for overflow or **ULONG_MIN** for
underflow, and the global variable **errno** is set to
ERANGE, indicating a range error. If no conversion
could take place, 0 is returned.

A related function is **strtol()**.

system

```
#include <stdlib.h>
int system(const char *str);
```

The **system()** function passes the string pointed to by *str*
as a command to the command processor of the
operating system.

If **system()** is called with a null pointer, it will return
nonzero if a command processor is present; 0 otherwise.
(Remember, some C++ code will be executed in
dedicated systems that do not have operating systems
and command processors.) The return value of **system()**
is implementation defined. However, generally it will
return 0 if the command was successfully executed,
nonzero otherwise.

A related function is **exit()**.

va_arg, va_start, and va_end

```
#include <stdarg.h>
void va_arg(va_list argptr, type);
va_start(va_list argptr, last_parm);
void va_end(va_list argptr);
```

The **va_arg()** , **va_start()**, and **va_end()** macros work together to allow a variable number of arguments to be passed to a function. The most common example of a function that takes a variable number of arguments is **printf()**. The type **va_list** is defined by STDARG.H.

The general procedure for creating a function that can take a variable number of arguments is as follows. The function must have at least one known parameter, but may have more, prior to the variable parameter list. The rightmost known parameter is called the *last_parm*. Before any of the variable-length parameters may be accessed, the argument pointer *argptr* must be initialized through a call to **va_start()**. After that, parameters are returned via calls to **va_arg()**, with *type* being the type of the next parameter. Finally, once all the parameters have been read and prior to returning from the function, a call to **va_end()** must be made to ensure that the stack is properly restored. If **va_end()** is not called, a program crash is very likely.

A related function is **vprintf()**.

The C++ Class-Based I/O System

In addition to supporting all of C's I/O system, C++ also defines its own class-based I/O system. Also like C's I/O system, C++'s I/O system is fully integrated. That is, the different aspects of C++'s I/O system, such as console I/O and disk I/O, are actually just different perspectives on the same mechanism. The advantage to using C++'s class-based I/O system is that it provides complete support for object-oriented programming and can operate upon user-defined objects.

The Basic Stream Classes

C++ provides support for its I/O system in the header file IOSTREAM.H. In this file a class hierarchy that supports I/O operations is defined. The lowest level class is called **streambuf**. This class provides the basic input and output operations. It is used primarily as a base class for other classes. (Unless you are deriving your own I/O classes, you will not use **streambuf** directly.)

The class **ios** is the base class of the class hierarchy that you will typically use when using the C++ I/O system. It provides formatting, error checking, and status information. From **ios** are derived several classes—sometimes through intermediary classes. The classes derived either directly or indirectly from **ios** that your program will generally interact with are listed here:

Class	Purpose
istream	General input
ostream	General output
iostream	General input/output
ifstream	File input
ofstream	File output
fstream	File input/output
istrstream	Array-based input
ostrstream	Array-based output
strstream	Array-based input/output

Remember   The **ios** class forms the base class for all of the C++ I/O that your program will typically use, and any class derived from it has access to many member functions and variables that control or monitor the fundamental operation of a stream.

C++'s Predefined Streams

When a C++ program begins execution, four built-in streams are automatically opened. They are listed here:

Stream	Meaning	Default Device
cin	Standard input	Keyboard
cout	Standard output	Screen
cerr	Standard error output	Screen
clog	Buffered version of cerr	Screen

By default, the standard streams are used to commuicate with the console. However, in environments that support I/O redirection (such as DOS, UNIX, and OS/2), the standard streams can be redirected to other devices or files.

The Format Flags

In the C++ I/O system, each stream has associated with it a set of format flags that control the way information is formatted by a stream. In **ios** the following enumeration is defined. The values defined by this enumeration are used to set or clear format flags.

```
// formatting flags
enum, {
  skipws = 0x0001,
  left = 0x0002,
  right = 0x0004,
  internal = 0x0008,
  dec = 0x0010,
  oct = 0x0020,
  hex = 0x0040,
  showbase = 0x0080,
  showpoint = 0x0100,
  uppercase = 0x0200,
  showpos = 0x0400,
  scientific = 0x0800,
  fixed = 0x1000,
  unitbuf = 0x2000,
  stdio = 0x4000
};
```

When the **skipws** flag is set, leading whitespace characters (spaces, tabs, and newlines) are discarded when performing input on a stream. When **skipws** is cleared, whitespace characters are not discarded.

When the **left** flag is set, output is left justified. When **right** is set, output is right justified. When the **internal** flag is set, a numeric value is padded to fill a field by inserting spaces between any sign or base character. If none of these flags is set, output is right justified by default.

By default, numeric values are output in decimal. However, it is possible to change the number base. Setting the **oct** flag causes output to be displayed in octal. Setting the **hex** flag causes output to be displayed in hexadecimal. To return output to decimal, set the **dec** flag.

Setting **showbase** causes the base of numeric values to be shown. For example, if the conversion base is hexadecimal, the value 1F will be displayed as 0x1F.

By default, when scientific notation is displayed, the e is in lowercase. Also, when a hexadecimal value is displayed, the x is in lowercase. When **uppercase** is set, these characters are displayed in uppercase.

Setting **showpos** causes a leading plus sign to be displayed before positive values.

Setting **showpoint** causes a decimal point and trailing zeros to be displayed for all floating point output—whether needed or not.

By setting the **scientific** flag, floating point numeric values are displayed using scientific notation. When **fixed** is set, floating point values are displayed using normal notation. By default, when **fixed** is set, six decimal places are displayed. When neither flag is set, the compiler chooses an appropriate method.

When **unitbuf** is set, the C++ I/O system performance is improved because output is partially buffered. When set, the buffer is flushed after each insertion operation.

When **stdio** is set, each stream is flushed after each output. Flushing a stream causes output to actually be written to the physical device linked to the stream.

The format flags are stored in a **long** integer and may be set by various member functions of the **ios** class.

The I/O Manipulators

In addition to setting or clearing the format flags directly, there is another way in which you may alter the format parameters of a stream. This second way is through the use of special functions called *manipulators*, which can be included in an I/O expression. The standard manipulators are shown in the following table:

Manipulator	Purpose	Input/Output
dec	Format numeric data in decimal	Output
endl	Output a newline character and flush the stream	Output
ends	Output a null	Output
flush	Flush a stream	Output
hex	Format numeric data in hexadecimal	Output
oct	Format numeric data in octal	Output
resetiosflags (long *f*)	Turn off the flags specified in *f*	Input and output

Manipulator	Purpose	Input/Output
setbase(int *base*)	Set the number base to *base*	Output
setfill(int *ch*)	Set the fill character to *ch*	Output
setiosflags (long *f*)	Turn on the flags specified in *f*	Input and output
setprecision (int *p*)	Set the number of digits displayed after a decimal point	Output
setw(int *w*)	Set the field width to *w*	Output
ws	Skip leading white space	Input

To access manipulators that take parameters, such as **setw()**, you must include IOMANIP.H in your program.

Creating Your Own Manipulator Functions

You can create your own manipulator functions. As you know, there are two basic types of manipulators: those that operate on input streams and those that operate on output streams. However, in addition to these two broad categories there is a secondary division: those manipulators that take an argument and those that don't. There are some significant differences between the way a parameterless manipulator is created and the way a parameterized manipulator is created.

All parameterless manipulator output functions have
this skeleton:

```
ostream &manip-name(ostream &stream)
{
  // your code here

  return stream;
}
```

Here, *manip-name* is the name of the manipulator.
Notice that a reference to a stream of type **ostream** is
returned. This is necessary if a manipulator is to be used
as part of a larger I/O expression. It is important to
understand that even though the manipulator has as its
single argument a reference to the stream upon which it
is operating, no argument is used when the manipulator
is inserted in an output operation.

All parameterless input manipulator functions have this
skeleton:

```
istream &manip-name(istream &stream)
{
  // your code here

  return stream;
}
```

An input manipulator recieves a reference to the stream
for which it was invoked. This stream must be returned
by the manipulator.

It is crucial that your manipulator return *stream*. If this is
not done, your manipulator cannot be used in a series of
input or output operations.

Creating a parameterized manipulator function is less
straightforward than creating manipulators that don't

have parameters. First, to create a parameterized manipulator, you must include IOMANIP.H. In IOMANIP.H is defined the class **OMANIP**, which is used to create output manipulators that take an argument. IOMANIP.H defines the class **IMANIP**, which is used to create parameterized input manipulators.

In general, whenever you need to create a manipulator that takes an argument, you will need to create two overloaded manipulator functions. In one, you need to define two parameters. The first parameter is a reference to the stream, and the second is the parameter that will be passed to the function. The second version of the manipulator defines only one parameter, which is the one specified when the manipulator is used in an I/O expression. This second version of the manipulator is used to generate a call to the first version. In general for output manipulators, you will use these general forms for creating parameterized manipulators:

ostream &*manip-name*(ostream &*stream, type param*)
{
  // your code here
  return *stream;*
}

// Overload
OMANIP (*type*) *manip-name*(*type param*) {
  return OMANIP (*type*) (*manip-name, param*);
}

Here, *type* specifies the type of parameter used by the manipulator. By default, you may only use types **int** and **long** for *type*.

If you want to use a different type of parameter, you must first tell the compiler about it using the

IOMANIPdeclare macro (defined in IOMANIP.H), as shown here:

IOMANIPdeclare(*type*);

Here, *type* is the type of the parameter that you want your manipulator to have.

The C++ Class-Based I/O Functions

The C++ class-based I/O functions contained or derived from the **ios** class are described here. These are the functions most commonly used in a C++ application. (Most of the I/O classes include member functions that are designed for use only when customizing the I/O system and are not used by the vast majority of application programs. For this reason, these functions are not described in this pocket reference.)

In many cases, the I/O functions are overloaded. In these cases, each version of the function is shown.

bad

```
#include <iostream.h>
int bad();
```

The **bad()** function is a member of **ios.**

The **bad()** function returns true if a fatal I/O error has occurred in the associated stream; otherwise, 0 is returned.

clear

```
#include <iostream.h>
void clear(int flags = 0);
```

The **clear()** function is a member of **ios**.

The **clear()** function clears the status flags associated with a stream. If *flags* is 0 (as it is by default), then all error flags are cleared (reset to 0). Otherwise, the status flags will be set to whatever value is specified in *flags*.

A related function is **rdstate()**.

eatwhite

```
#include <iostream.h>
void eatwhite();
```

The **eatwhite()** function is a member of **istream()**.

The **eatwhite()** function reads and discards all leading white space from the associated input stream and advances the get pointer to the first non-whitespace character.

A related function is **ignore()**.

eof

```
#include <iostream.h>
int eof();
```

The **eof()** function is a member of **ios**.

The **eof()** function returns true when the end of the associated input file has been encountered; otherwise it returns 0.

Related functions are **bad()**, **fail()**, **good()**, **rdstate()**, and **clear()**.

fail

```
#include <iostream.h>
int fail();
```

The **fail()** function is a member of **ios**.

The **fail()** function returns true if an I/O error has occurred in the associated stream. Otherwise, it returns 0.

Related functions are **good()**, **eof()**, **bad()**, **clear()**, and **rdstate()**.

fill

```
#include <iostream.h>
char fill();
char fill(char ch);
```

The **fill()** function is a member of **ios**.

By default, when a field needs to be filled, it is filled with spaces. However, you can specify the fill character using the **fill()** function and specifying the new fill character in ch. The old fill character is returned.

To obtain the current fill character, use the first form of **fill()**, which returns the current fill character.

Related functions are **precision()** and **width()**.

flags

```
#include <iostream.h>
long flags();
long flags(long f);
```

The **flags()** function is a member of **ios.**

The first form of **flags()** simply returns the current format flags settings of the associated stream.

The second form of **flags()** sets all format flags associated with a stream as specified by *f*. When you use this version, the bit pattern found in *f* is copied into the format flags associated with the stream. This version also returns the previous settings.

Related functions are **unsetf()** and **setf()**.

flush

```
#include <iostream.h>
ostream &flush();
```

The **flush()** function is a member of **ostream**.

The **flush()** function causes the buffer connected to the associated output stream to be physically written to the device. The function returns a reference to its associated stream.

Related functions are **put()** and **write()**.

fstream, ifstream, and ofstream

```
#include <fstream.h>
fstream();
fstream(const char *filename, int mode,
     int access=filebuf::openprot);
fstream(int fd);
fstream(int fd, char *buf, int size);

ifstream();
ifstream(const char *filename,
      int mode=ios::in,
      int access=filebuf::openprot);
ifstream(int fd);
ifstream(int fd, char *buf, int size);

ofstream();
ofstream(const char *filename,
      int mode=ios::out,
      int access=filebuf::openprot);
ofstream(int fd);
ofstream(int fd, char *buf, int size);
```

The **fstream()**, **ifstream()**, and **ofstream()** are the constructors of the **fstream**, **ifstream**, and **ofstream** classes, respectively.

The versions of **fstream()**, **ifstream()**, and **ofstream()** that take no parameters create a stream that is not associated with any file. This stream can then be linked to a file using **open()**.

The versions of **fstream()**, **ifstream()**, and **ofstream()** that take a filename for their first parameters are the most commonly used in application programs. Although it is entirely proper to open a file using the **open()**

function, most of the time you will not do so because these **ifstream**, **ofstream**, and **fstream** constructor functions automatically open the file when the stream is created. The constructor functions have the same parameters and defaults as the **open()** function. (See **open** for details.) Therefore, the most common way you will see a file opened is shown in this example:

```
ifstream mystream("myfile");
```

If for some reason the file cannot be opened, the value of the associated stream variable will be 0. Therefore, whether you use a constructor function to open the file or an explicit call to **open()**, you will want to confirm that the file has actually been opened by testing the value of the stream.

The versions of **fstream()**, **ifstream()**, and **ofstream()** that take only one parameter, an already valid file descriptor, create a stream and then associate that stream with the file descriptor specified in *fd*.

The versions of **fstream()**, **ifstream()**, and **ofstream()** that take a file descriptor, a pointer to a buffer, and a size create a stream and associate it with the file descriptor specified in *fd*. *buf* must be a pointer to memory that will serve as a buffer, and *size* specifies the length of the buffer, in bytes. (If *buf* is null and/or if *size* is 0, no buffering takes place.)

Related functions are **close()** and **open()**.

gcount

```
#include <iostream.h>
int gcount();
```

The **gcount()** function is a member of **istream**.

The **gcount()** function returns the number of characters read by the last input operation.

Related functions are **get()**, **getline()**, and **read()**.

get

```
#include <iostream.h>
int get();
istream &get(char &ch);
istream &get(char *buf, int num,
          char delim = '\n');
istream &get(streambuf &buf,
          char delim = '\n');
```

The **get()** function is a member of **istream**.

In general, **get()** reads characters from an input stream. The parameterless form of **get()** reads a single character from the associated stream and returns that value.

The form of **get()** that takes a single character reference reads a character from the associated stream and puts that value in *ch*. It returns a reference to the stream. (Note that *ch* may also be of type **unsigned char *** or **signed char ***.)

The form of **get()** that takes three parameters reads characters into the array pointed to by *buf* until either *num* characters have been read or the character specified by *delim* has been encountered. The array pointed to by *buf* will be null terminated by **get()**. If no *delim* parameter is specified, by default a newline character acts as a delimiter. If the delimiter character is encountered in the input stream it is *not* extracted.

Instead, it remains in the stream until the next input operation. This function returns a reference to the stream. (Note that *buf* may also be of type **unsigned char *** or **signed char ***.)

The form of **get()** that takes two parameters reads characters from the input stream into the **streambuf** (or derived) object. Characters are read until the specified delimiter is encountered. It returns a reference to the stream.

Related functions are **put()**, **read()**, and **getline()**.

getline

```
#include <iostream.h>
istream &getline(char *buf, int num,
                 char delim = '\n');
```

The **getline()** function is a member of **istream**.

The **getline()** function reads characters into the array pointed to by *buf* until either *num* characters have been read or the character specified by *delim* has been encountered. The array pointed to by *buf* will be null terminated by **getline()**. If no *delim* parameter is specified, by default a newline character acts as a delimiter. If the delimiter character is encountered in the input stream it is extracted, but is not put into *buf*. This function returns a reference to the stream. (Note that *buf* may also be of type **unsigned char *** or **signed char ***.)

Related functions are **get()** and **read()**.

good

```
#include <iostream.h>
int good();
```

The **good()** function is a member of **ios**.

The **good()** function returns true if no I/O errors have occurred in the associated stream; otherwise, it returns 0.

Related functions are **bad()**, **fail()**, **eof()**, **clear()**, and **rdstate()**.

ignore

```
#include <iostream.h>
istream &ignore(int num = 1, int delim = EOF);
```

The **ignore()** function is a member of **istream**.

You can use the **ignore()** member function to read and discard characters from the input stream. It reads and discards characters until either *num* characters have been ignored (1 by default) or until the character specified by *delim* is encountered (**EOF** by default). If the delimiting character is encountered, it is removed from the input stream. The function returns a reference to the stream.

Related functions are **get()** and **getline()**.

open

```
#include <fstream.h>
void open(const char *filename, int mode,
          int access=filebuf::openprot);
```

The **open()** function is a member of **fstream**, **ifstream**, and **ofstream**.

A file is associated with a stream by using the **open()** function. Here, *filename* is the name of the file, which may include a path specifier. The value of *mode* determines how the file is opened. It must be one (or more) of these values:

ios::app
ios::ate
ios::binary
ios::in
ios::nocreate
ios::noreplace
ios::out
ios::trunc

You can combine two or more of these values by ORing them together.

Including **ios::app** causes all output to that file to be appended to the end. This value can only be used with files capable of output. Including **ios::ate** causes a seek to the end of the file to occur when the file is opened. Although **ios::ate** causes a seek to the end-of-file, I/O operations can still occur anywhere within the file.

The **ios::binary** value causes the file to be opened for binary I/O operations. By default, files are opened in text mode.

The **ios::in** value specifies that the file is capable of input. The **ios::out** value specifies that the file is capable of output. However, creating a stream using **ifstream** implies input, and creating a stream using **ofstream** implies output, so in these cases, it is unnecessary to supply these values.

Including **ios::nocreate** causes the **open()** function to fail if the file does not already exist. The **ios::noreplace** value causes the **open()** function to fail if the file does already exist.

The **ios::trunc** value causes the contents of a preexisting file by the same name to be destroyed and the file is truncated to zero length.

The value of *access* determines how the file can be accessed. Its default value is **filebuf::openprot** (**filebuf** is a base class of the file classes), which is 0x644 for UNIX environments, and means a normal file. In DOS environments, the *access* value generally corresponds to DOS's file attribute codes. They are

Attribute	Meaning
0	Normal file—open access
1	Read-only file
2	Hidden file
4	System file
8	Archive bit set

You can OR two or more of these together. For DOS, a normal file has an *access* value of 0. For other operating systems, check your compiler's user manual for the valid values of *access*.

When opening a file, both *mode* and *access* will default. When opening an input file, *mode* will default to **ios::in**. When opening an output file, *mode* will default to **ios::out**. In either case, the default for *access* is a normal file. For example, this opens a file called TEST for output:

```
out.open("test");
// defaults to output and normal file
```

To open a stream for input and output, you must specify both the **ios::in** and the **ios::out** *mode* values, as shown here:

```
mystream.open("test", ios::in | ios::out);
```

No default value for *mode* is supplied when opening read/write files.

In all cases, if **open()** fails, the stream will be 0. Therefore, before using a file, you should test to make sure that the open operation succeeded.

Related functions are **close()**, **fstream()**, **ifstream()**, and **ofstream()**.

peek

```
#include <iostream.h>
int peek();
```

The **peek()** function is a member of **istream**.

The **peek()** function returns the next character in the stream or **EOF** if the end of the file is encountered. It does not, under any circumstances, remove the character from the stream.

A related function is **get()**.

precision

```
#include <iostream.h>
int precision();
int precision(int p);
```

The **precision()** function is a member of **ios.**

By default, six digits are displayed after the decimal point when floating point values are output. However, using the second form of **precision()** you can set this number to the value specified in p. The original value is returned.

The first version of **precision()** returns the current value.

Related functions are **width()** and **fill()**.

put

```
#include <iostream.h>
ostream &put(char ch);
```

The **put()** function is a member of **ostream.**

The **put()** function writes ch to the associated output stream. It returns a reference to the stream.

Related functions are **write()** and **get()**.

putback

```
#include <iostream.h>
istream &putback(char ch);
```

The **putback()** function is a member of **istream**.

The **putback()** function returns *ch* to the associated input stream.

Note *ch* must be the last character read from that stream.

A related function is **peek()**.

rdstate

```
#include <iostream.h>
int rdstate();
```

The **rdstate()** function is a member of **ios**.

The **rdstate()** function returns the status of the associated stream. The C++ I/O system maintains status information about the outcome of each I/O operation relative to each active stream. The current state of the I/O system is held in an integer, in which the following flags are encoded:

Name	Meaning
goodbit	0 when no errors occur 1 when an error is flagged
eofbit	1 when end-of-file is encountered 0 otherwise

Name	Meaning
failbit	1 when a nonfatal I/O error has occurred 0 otherwise
badbit	1 when a fatal I/O error has occurred 0 otherwise

These flags are enumerated inside **ios**.

rdstate() returns 0 when no error has occurred; otherwise, an error bit has been set.

Related functions are **eof()**, **good()**, **bad()**, **clear()**, and **fail()**.

read

```
#include <iostream.h>
istream &read(char *buf, int num);
```

The **read()** function is a member of **istream**.

The **read()** function reads *num* bytes from the associated input stream and puts them in the buffer pointed to by *buf* (note that *buf* may also be of type **unsigned char *** or **signed char ***). If the end of the file is reached before *num* characters has been read, **read()** simply stops, and the buffer contains as many characters as were available. It returns a reference to the stream.

Related functions are **get()**, **getline()**, and **write()**.

seekg

```
#include <iostream.h>
istream &seekg(streamoff offset,
               ios::seek_dir origin)
```

```
istream &seekg(streampos position);

ostream &seekp(streamoff offset,
               ios::seek_dir origin);
ostream &seekp(streampos position);
```

The **seekg()** function is a member of **istream**, and the **seekp()** function is a member of **ostream**.

In C++'s I/O system, you perform random access using the **seekg()** and **seekp()** functions. To this end, the C++ I/O system manages two pointers associated with a file. One is the *get pointer*, which specifies where in the file the next input operation will occur. The other is the *put pointer*, which specifies where in the file the next output operation will occur. Each time an input or an output operation takes place, the appropriate pointer is automatically sequentially advanced. However, using the **seekg()** and **seekp()** functions, it is possible to access the file in a nonsequential fashion.

The two-parameter version of **seekg()** moves the get pointer *offset* number of bytes from the location specified by *origin*. The two-parameter version of **seekp()** moves the put pointer *offset* number of bytes from the location specified by *origin*. The *offset* is of type **streamoff**, which is defined in IOSTREAM.H. A **streamoff** object is capable of containing the largest valid value that *offset* can have.

The *origin* is of type **ios::seek_dir** and is an enumeration that has these values:

ios::beg	Seek from beginning
ios::cur	Seek from current position
ios::end	Seek from end

The single-parameter versions of **seekg()** and **seekp()** move the file pointers to the location specified by *position*. This value must have been previously obtained using a call to either **tellg()** or **tellp()**, respectively. **streampos** is a type defined in IOSTREAM.H that is capable of containing the largest valid value that *position* can have. These functions return a reference to the associated stream.

Related functions are **tellg()** and **tellp()**.

setf

```
#include <iostream.h>
long setf(long flags);
long setf(long flags1, long flags2);
```

The **setf()** function is a member of **ios**.

The first version of **setf()** turns on the format flags specified by *flags*. (All other flags are unaffected.) For example, to turn on the **showpos** flag, you can use this statement:

```
stream.setf(ios::showpos);
```

Here, *stream* is the stream you wish to affect.

It is important to understand that a call to **setf()** is done relative to a specific stream. There is no concept of calling **setf()** by itself. Put differently, there is no concept in C++ of global format status. Each stream maintains its own format status information individually.

When you want to set more than one flag, you can OR together the values of the flags you want set.

Reminder   Because the format flags are defined within the **ios** class, you must access their values by using **ios**

and the scope resolution operator. For example,
showbase by itself will not be recognized. You must
specify **ios::showbase**.

The second version of **setf()** affects only the flags that
are set in *flags2*. The corresponding flags are first reset
and then set according to the flags specified by *flags1*. It
is important to understand that even if *flags1* contains
other set flags not specified by *flags2*, only those
specified by *flags2* will be affected.

Since it is common to refer to the **oct**, **dec**, and **hex**
fields, they can be collectively referred to as
ios::basefield. Similarly, the **left**, **right**, and **internal**
fields can be referred to as **ios::adjustfield**. Finally, the
scientific and **fixed** fields can be referenced as
ios::floatfield.

Both versions of **setf()** return the previous settings of the
format flags associated with the stream.

Related functions are **unsetf()** and **flags()**.

setmode

```
#include <fstream.h>
int setmode(int mode = filebuf::text);
```

The **setmode()** function is a member of **ofstream** and
ifstream.

The **setmode()** function sets the mode of the associated
stream to either binary or text. (Text is the default.) The
valid values for *mode* are **filebuf::text** and
filebuf::binary.

The function returns the previous mode setting or −1 if an error occurs.

A related function is **open()**.

str

```
#include <strstream.h>
char *str();
```

The **str()** function is a member of **strstream.**

The **str()** function "freezes" a dynamically allocated input array and returns a pointer to it. Once a dynamic array is frozen, it may not be used for output again. Therefore, you will not want to freeze the array until you are through outputting characters to it.

Note   This function is for use with array-based I/O.

Related functions are **strstream()**, **istrstream()**, and **ostrstream()**.

strstream, istrstream, and ostrstream

```
#include <strstream.h>
strstream();
strstream(char *buf, int size, int mode);

istrstream(const char *buf);
istrstream(const char *buf, int size);
```

```
ostrstream();
ostrstream(char *buf, int size,
           int mode=ios::out)
```

The **strstream** constructor is a member of **strstream**, the **istrstream()** constructor is a member of **istrstream**, and the **ostrstream()** constructor is a member of **ostrstream**.

These constructors are used to create array-based streams that support C++'s array-based I/O functions.

For **ostrstream()**, *buf* is a pointer to the array that will be used to collect characters written to the stream. The size of the array is passed in the *size* parameter. By default, the stream is opened for normal output, but you can specify a different mode using the *mode* parameter. The legal values for *mode* are the same as those used with **open()**. For most purposes, *mode* will be allowed to default. If you use the parameterless version of **ostrstream()**, a dynamic array is automatically allocated.

For the single-parameter version of **istrstream()**, *buf* is a pointer to the array that will be used as a source of characters each time input is performed on the stream. The contents of the array pointed to by *buf* must be null terminated. However, the null terminator is never read from the array.

If you wish only part of a string to be used for input, use the two-parameter form of the **istrstream** constructor. Here, only the first *size* elements of the array pointed to by *buf* will be used. This string need not be null terminated, since it is the value of *size* that determines the size of the string.

To create an array-based stream capable of input and output, use **strstream()**. In the parameterized version, *buf* points to the string that will be used for I/O operations. The value of *size* specifies the size of the array. The value of *mode* determines how the stream operates. For normal input/output operations, *mode* will be **ios::in | ios::out**. For input, the array must be null terminated.

If you use the parameterless version of **strstream()**, the buffer used for I/O will be dynamically allocated, and the mode is set for read/write operations.

Related functions are **str()** and **open()**.

sync_with_stdio

```
#include <iostream.h>
static void sync_with_stdio();
```

The **sync_with_stdio()** function is a member of **ios**.

Calling **sync_with_stdio()** allows the standard C-like I/O system to be safely used concurrently with the C++ class-based I/O system.

tellg and tellp

```
#include <iostream.h>
streampos tellg();
streampos tellp():
```

The **tellg()** function is a member of **istream**, and **tellp()** is a member of **ostream**.

The C++ I/O system manages two pointers associated with a file. One is the *get pointer*, which specifies where in the file the next input operation will occur. The other is the *put pointer*, which specifies where in the file the next output operation will occur. Each time an input or an output operation takes place, the appropriate pointer is automatically sequentially advanced. You can determine the current position of the get pointer using **tellg()** and of the put pointer using **tellp()**.

streampos is a type defined in IOSTREAM.H that is capable of holding the largest value that either function can return.

The values returned by **tellg()** and **tellp()** can be used as parameters to **seekg()** and **seekp()**, respectively.

Related functions are **seekg()** and **seekp()**.

unsetf

```
#include <iostream.h>
long unsetf(long flags);
```

The **unsetf()** function is a member of **ios**.

The **unsetf()** function is used to clear one or more format flags.

The flags specified by *flags* are cleared. (All other flags are unaffected.) The previous flag settings are returned.

Related functions are **setf()** and **flags()**.

width

```
#include <iostream.h>
int width();
int width(int w);
```

The **width()** function is a member of **ios**.

To obtain the current field width, use the first form of **width()**. This version returns the current field width.

To set the field width use the second form. Here, *w* becomes the field width, and the previous field width is returned.

Related functions are **precision()** and **fill()**.

write

```
#include <iostream.h>
ostream &write(const char *buf, int num);
```

The **write()** function is a member of **ostream**.

The **write()** function writes *num* bytes to the associated output stream from the buffer pointed to by *buf*. (Note that *buf* may also be of type **unsigned char *** or **signed char ***.) It returns a reference to the stream.

Related functions are **read()** and **put()**.

A Short Note About the Old Stream Class Library

When C++ was first invented, a smaller and slightly different I/O class library was created. This library is defined in the file STREAM.H. However, when C++

specification 2.0 was released by AT&T, the I/O library was enhanced and was put in the file IOSTREAM.H. Most C++ compilers still support the old stream library for the sake of compatibility with older C++ programs. However, you should use the IOSTREAM library when writing new programs.